RUBBLE NATION

Haiti's Pain,
Haiti's Promise

D1412203

Text by Chris Herlinger
Photographs and Afterword by Paul Jeffrey

Seabury Books
NEW YORK

Portions of this book originally appeared, in different form, in *The Christian Century, National Catholic Reporter, New World Outlook, Presbyterians Today, Response,* and in Catholic News Service and Ecumenical News International.

Library of Congress Cataloging-in-Publication Data

Herlinger, Chris.
Rubble nation : Haiti's pain, Haiti's promise / by Chris Herlinger ;
photographs by Paul Jeffrey.
p. cm.

ISBN 978-1-59627-228-6 (pbk.) -- ISBN 978-1-59627-229-3 (ebook)
1. Earthquake relief--Haiti. 2. Haiti Earthquake, Haiti, 2010. 3. Haiti--Economic conditions--21st century. 4. Haiti--Social conditions--21st century. 5. Haiti--Politics and government--21st century. I. Jeffrey, Paul. II. Title.
HV600 2010. H2 H47 2011
363.34'958097294--dc23

2011021255

Seabury Books
445 Fifth Avenue
New York, New York 10016
www.churchpublishing.org
An imprint of Church Publishing Incorporated

Printed in Canada

How much of what we did was good?
Everything seems to move beyond
Our remedy.

—Alice Goodman, libretto of *Nixon in China*

"Haiti was a land full of people without shoes, black people, whose feet walked the dusty roads to market in the early morning, or trod softly on the bare floors of hotels, serving foreign guests. Barefooted ones tending the rice and cane fields under the hot sun, climbing mountain slopes, baking coffee beans, wading through surf to fishing boats on the blue seas. All of the work that kept Haiti alive, paid the interest on American loans, and enriched foreign traders, was done by people without shoes."

— Langston Hughes, *I Wonder as I Wander*

"Lespwa fè viv." (Hope keeps one alive.)

—Haitian proverb

Contents

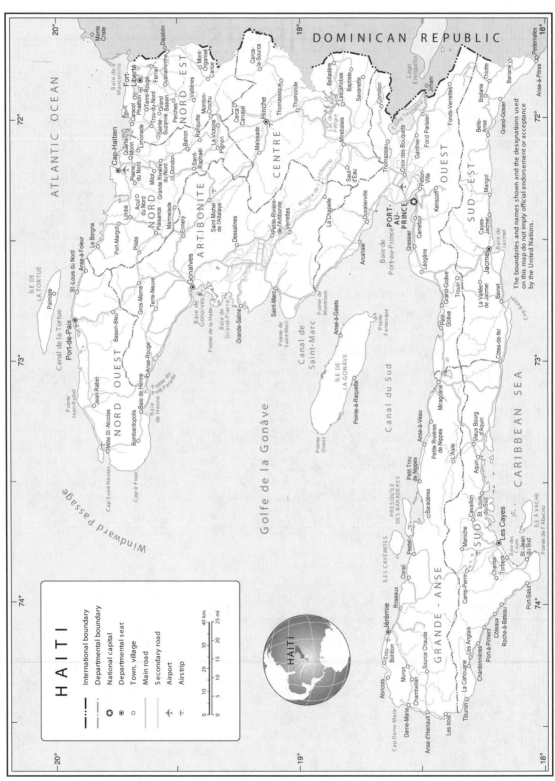

HAITI

- ···-··· International boundary
- ···-··· Departmental boundary
- ⊛ National capital
- ◉ Departmental seat
- ○ Town, village
- — Main road
- — Secondary road
- ✈ Airport
- ✢ Airstrip

0 10 20 30 40 km
0 5 10 15 20 25 mi

ATLANTIC OCEAN

DOMINICAN REPUBLIC

Monte Cristi

Baie de Mancenille

Fort-Liberté

Dajabón

NORD-EST

Mont-Organisé

Ouanaminthe

Cerca-la-Source

Carice

Ferrier

Phaéton

Terre-Rouge

Caracol

Quartier Morin

Limonade

Trou-du-Nord

Sainte-Suzanne

Grand Bassin

Ouanaminthe

Vallières

Mombin Crochu

Cap-Haïtien

Plaine du Nord

Milot

Acul du Nord

Grande Rivière du Nord

Dondon

Saint-Raphaël

Ranquitte

La Victoire

Pignon

Cerca Carvajal

Maïssade

Hinche

Thomassique

Belladère

Lascahobas

Savanette

Baptiste

Cornillon

Lac de Péligre

Mirebalais

NORD

Lumbé

Pilate

Plaisance

Marmelade

Ennery

Saint-Michel de l'Atalaye

Dessalines

ARTIBONITE

Petite-Rivière-de-l'Artibonite

Verrettes

La Chapelle

Rivière de l'Artibonite

CENTRE

Thomonde

Perches

Banon

Le Borgne

Port-Margot

Port-de-Paix

St-Louis du Nord

Anse-à-Foleur

ÎLE DE LA TORTUE

Palmiste

Canal de la Tortue

NORD-OUEST

Bassin-Bleu

Jean-Rabel

Baie de Henne

Bombardopolis

Môle St-Nicolas

Cap-à-Foux

Cap Saint-Nicolas

Windward Passage

Pointe Jean-Rabel

Gros-Morne

Terre-Neuve

Gonaïves

Baie de Gonaïves

Baie de Grand-Pierre

Grande-Saline

Saint-Marc

Pointe de Montrouis

Pointe de Saint-Marc

Canal de Saint-Marc

Anse-à-Galets

ÎLE DE LA GONÂVE

Pointe-à-Raquette

Golfe de la Gonâve

Pointe Ouest

Canal du Sud

Arcahaie

Baie de Port-au-Prince

Gressier

Léogâne

Carrefour

PORT-AU-PRINCE

Pétion-Ville

Kenscoff

Croix des Bouquets

Ganthier

Ford Parisien

Thomazeau

Saut d'Eau

Duvalierville

Étang Saumâtre

Lago Enriquillo

OUEST

Fonds-Verrettes

Jimaní

SUD-EST

Marigot

Cayes-Jacmel

Jacmel

Baie de Jacmel

Belle-Anse

Grand-Gosier

Bodarie

Thiotte

Banane

Pedernales

Anse-à-Pitres

Petit-Goâve

Grand-Goâve

Trouin

La Vallée de Jacmel

Bainet

Côtes-de-fer

Cap de Banet

Miragoâne

Anse-à-Veau

Vieux Bourg d'Aquin

Petite Rivière de Nippes

L'Asile

Aquin

Cavaillon

Maniche

St. Louis du Sud

St-Jean du Sud

SUD

Les Cayes

Baie des Cayes

Chantal

Torbeck

ÎLE A VACHE

Pointe de l'Abacou

PRESQU'ÎLE DES BARADÈRES

Petit Trou de Nippes

Baradères

Pestel

Corail

Roseaux

ÎLES CAYÉMITES

GRANDE-ANSE

Jérémie

Trou Bonbon

Abricots

Dame-Marie

Cap Dame-Marie

Anse d'Hainault

Les Irois

Moron

Chambellan

Camp-Perrin

Source Chaude

Tiburon

La Cahouane

Chardonnières

Port-à-Piment

Coteaux

Roche-à-Bateau

Les Anglais

Port-Salut

CARIBBEAN SEA

HAITI

The boundaries and names shown and the designations used on this map do not imply official endorsement or acceptance by the United Nations.

Department of Peacekeeping Operations
Cartographic Section

Map No. 3855 Rev. 2   UNITED NATIONS
January 2004

Acknowledgments

Books are collaborative efforts, something that needs repeating in this case, when much of what we did in Haiti would not have been possible without the help of so many others, Haitian and non-Haitian. A list of all of those who assisted us would take several pages and is beyond the scope of concise words of acknowledgement. (In the case of reporting and writing the text, that would mean thanking those who assisted during four separate assignments to Haiti: in January 2010, June and July 2010, January 2011, and April 2011.) We wish we could name them all here. Suffice it to say that many of them are mentioned in the text, and most are humanitarian workers who work for the member agencies of ACT Alliance or are themselves ACT Alliance staff.

A special word of thanks is due, however, to the staff of the Lutheran World Federation in Port-au-Prince who took us in during the initial days after the earthquake, and did so while they were experiencing their own personal grief and trauma. They were gallant and gracious beyond words. A word of thanks is also due to Louijeune Ulrick, who helped us both with translation and transportation while in Haiti.

Beyond that, Chris wishes to thank his U.S.- and Latin America–based Church World Service colleagues, and Aaron Tate and Burton Joseph, CWS staff members in Haiti. Davis Perkins of CPG supported this book from the beginning and Joan Castagnone was a patient and passionate editor. Elizabeth Haak brought her many editing talents to the project as well.

Much of the writing of this book occurred during several short residencies at the Collegeville Institute for Ecumenical and Cultural Research in Collegeville, Minnesota, a place very far from the realities of Haiti but which proved to be a nurturing and congenial home, thanks to its peaceful surroundings and wonderful staff. As always, a word of thanks, with love, respect, and affection, to many, many dear friends in so many places, and to the Denver bureau: David, Lynn, and Becky.

Paul would like to thank the people of Mizak, Port-au-Prince, Foret-des-pins, Embouchure, Port-de-Paix, Mare Rouge, Jacmel, Léogâne, and so many other places in Haiti for their dignity and hospitality. Mesi anpil!

We dedicate this book to the memory of those who died on January 12, 2010, and to the many Haitians who have courageously struggled for decades to construct a genuine democracy that embraces all, that celebrates Haitian culture, and that builds a sustainable and just future for Haiti's children.

Chris Herlinger, New York City
Paul Jeffrey, Eugene, Oregon

Introduction

Almost fourteen months to the day after Haiti suffered a 7.0-magnitude earthquake on January 12, 2010, that left as many as 230,000 people dead, Japan experienced the largest earthquake in its recorded history and one of the most powerful in the last century—an 8.9-magnitude event that may have killed some 23,000 people, roughly a tenth of the number who perished in Haiti.

There were, of course, horrible particularities about the 2011 Japan disaster—a resulting tsunami and the meltdown of several nuclear reactors—that had no parallel in Haiti and may yet have profound consequences for Japan and the world. Still, the events in Haiti and Japan invite comparison, prompting a simple and obvious question: why did a stronger earthquake cause far less damage in Japan than a weaker earthquake in Haiti? The answer is rooted in the vulnerability of Haiti: its poverty, weak government, dependence on outside assistance—all linked to its decades-long dominance and defilement by outside powers.

Rabbi Brent Spodek, then the rabbi-in-residence at American Jewish World Service, a New York–based humanitarian organization, reflected on the Haitian experience for an agency magazine just prior to the first anniversary of the Haiti quake. He argued that the severity of what happened in Haiti was not because "the earth shook so hard, but because the human structures built on it were so flimsy." While it is human nature to ask the question why "God caused the earth to shudder," Spodek argued an ultimately more productive question to ask, is "what we were doing on January 11—and the days, months and years before that—when Haiti was already the poorest country in the Western Hemisphere?" He continues,

> Thousands upon thousands of people died because of human indifference to Haitian suffering before the quake, not the tremors of the earth on January 12th. Why did we allow a city and a country to be built in such a way that hundreds of thousands of people died when the earth shook? That is the more frightening question, because an honest reckoning might require that we acknowledge our own responsibility for human suffering.

That recognition of responsibility is what we mean when we speak of Haiti's pain. The earthquake that ravaged Haiti didn't just open up the ground, though it did that; it also exposed the fault lines of a long-damaged society, a society that in many ways was a "Rubble Nation" long before the earthquake. Haiti is, as Dominican-American writer Junot Díaz has called it, "the third world's third world. Haiti is by nearly every metric one of the poorest nations on the planet—a mind-blowing 80 percent of the population live in poverty, and 54 percent live in what is called 'abject poverty.'"

The history of why this is so was easy to ignore in the wake of the earthquake. It is as if history seemingly began with the shaking on the afternoon of January 12, 2010—the legacy of slavery, several U.S. military occupations, ruinous agricultural and economic policies, and outside support for corrupt governments and repression against popular movements hardly mattered. While the well-meaning, well-intended, and certainly well-funded rush to assist Haiti was understandable and admirable, too little time was spent in recognizing *why* the Haitian state was weak, *why* the unresolved issues raised by the brutal rule of the Duvaliers and the subsequent administrations of Jean-Bertrand Aristide still mattered. They mattered because the terrible weight of history pressed down with particular vengeance on Haiti. That was, and remains, Haiti's pain.

And yet Haiti's strength—its promise—was always, and remains, its people. It became standard after the quake to talk about the resilience and strength of Haiti's populace, so much so that it bordered on cliché to keep reiterating the point. Yet the bravery, courage, and yes, endurance and fortitude, of Haitians saved lives, kept the country going through the difficult months of 2010 and 2011, and will continue to do so well into the future. But this can only happen if people of good will, particularly in the United States, recognize that a reordering of relations with Haiti is desperately needed. Speaking as a U.S. citizen, health and human rights activist Paul Farmer declared two decades ago that we need a "candid and careful assessment of our ruinous policies toward Haiti." That may require, Farmer suggested, remorse and reckoning—two things that are never easy in the history between peoples:

> But for many, old-fashioned penitence might be the first step toward a new solidarity, a pragmatic solidarity that could supplant both our malignant policies of the past and the well-meaning but unfocused charity that does not respond to Haitian aspirations. The Haitian people are asking not for charity, but for justice.

In the weeks after the quake, Denisse Pichardo, who runs a Dominican-based humanitarian group that has worked to improve relations between the two peoples who share the island of Hispañola, echoed those themes, placing them in the context of the remarkable outpouring of international support for Haiti following January 12, 2010. "We all have debts to Haiti," she argued, beginning with the French, continuing with the U.S. military occupation and years of U.S. support for Haitian dictatorships. Her own country—which acted most admirably in responding first to Haiti's needs after the quake—also has many debts to Haiti, with its history of exploitation of Haitian workers. "We've seen Haitians as less valuable than people of other countries," she said of the world in general. "We don't, and haven't, valued them as people. We never think what we can do together with Haitians. We don't learn their language. But somehow we need to walk together with them."

Rubble Nation: Haiti's Pain, Haiti's Promise is an attempt, in text and photographs, by two journalists who work for faith-based humanitarian agencies to explore what that means, in the hope that someday, in the global imagination, Haiti's potential and promise will be heralded more than Haiti's penury and pain.

1

Rubble Nation

Port-au-Prince is a city of jagged edges—of potholes and glass, of exposed wires and pipes, of open sewers and rotting mango peelings, of sludge, dirt, and mud. The edges are most visible in midday when the sun is at its height and the contrasts of glaring sun and dark skin, of light walls and shadowed alleyways, are most striking. So it comes as a relief when the softening afternoon light begins to slide slowly into twilight, as it did at 4:53 p.m. on January 12, 2010.

On that day, high up in Port-au-Prince's hilly Delmas neighborhood, Anouk Noël and her younger sister, Rode, were in their house, starting to think about dinner. Anouk had not been well in the week since her twenty-ninth birthday on January 5, but she was feeling better—well enough, anyway, to think about going out the next day and have her photograph taken by a professional as a belated birthday gift. Such outings are special to Anouk; she suffers from dwarfism and needs family members to carry her because she cannot walk.

Anouk and Rode knew right away that the vibrations they felt were ominous. Port-au-Prince had experienced tremors before, but these became horrifying—the sisters' house was swaying and the two heard loud, low rumbles, sounding like bullets and breaking glass. Later, others described the racket as *goudougoudou*—a vernacular Kreyòl term describing the sound of the quake that came to mean the earthquake itself. Frightened by the sharp vibrations, Rode fled, along with the sisters' mother, Melanie, and brother, Jimmy, just as the six-story building next door collapsed onto her family's house. Though momentarily relieved to be outside, a dazed Rode panicked when she remembered that her sister was still in the damaged house. She ran back, saw her sister, who had passed out, and carried her through the debris and onto the street. There the two met their mother and brother; Jimmy had injured his foot, but not seriously. The family stood amid glass and dust, dirt and fallen concrete; rubble from the collapsed house next door buried members of several families. A year later, a visiting construction engineer

1

wondered if bodies were still concealed under the dusty wreckage of gray concrete and white plaster. "This is crazy," he said. "We might be walking over people right now."

Up the hill from Delmas, Astrid Nissen, a German humanitarian worker, was at her desk working on a budget proposal for her agency, Diakonie Katastrophenhilfe, when the roaring began. She heard her Haitian colleagues shouting "earthquake, earthquake." They fell to the floor, praying. The swaying was surreal, she recalled, but the building withstood it. Once Nissen collected herself, still shaking and trembling, she called a colleague in Colombia and told her that Port-au-Prince had just been struck by an earthquake. It was the last international phone call Nissen would make for a while. After collecting her shoes, her cigarettes ("I needed them"), and reuniting with her partner, Jean Gardy Marius, a Haitian physician, Nissen spent the next eight hours fielding calls on Skype, giving interviews, but not sure precisely what to say. At first she thought, hope against hope, that "it couldn't be that bad." But over the hours, the news worsened: perhaps the most ominous signal of the quake's magnitude was the fact that the National Palace had collapsed. Early on, Nissen went downtown, where some of the worst damage had occurred, and kept muttering, as if in a daze, "It isn't true. It isn't true." But it *was* true— corpses littered the street, bodies were scattered on the sidewalk. Things only got worse in the following days: Marius's sister was among the victims, and bodies continued to line the road—eventually the sight of corpses being lifted onto the backs of trucks for burial became commonplace. For weeks afterward, packs of barking dogs roamed the streets at night, looking for flesh.

On that first night, it was dark by 5:30, and the streets were packed with people walking uphill because they feared a tsunami. Many were covered with dust, and everywhere, Nissen recalls, "it smelled like burning tires." Other, more pungent smells would emerge within days. Immediately following the quake, one had to be careful when driving—the roads were packed with "people, people, people," especially at night, since so many people were sleeping on the streets.

At 4:53 p.m., January 12, 2011, a year to the moment after the quake occurred, Nissen looked up at the gentle, clear blue sky of dusk, and said, "Life goes on."

It does, and it did. The Noël family, shaken and scared but without serious injuries, had to make some tough decisions, like where to go, what to do with their damaged home, what to do about money. The home had to be abandoned, at least for the moment; the family did not know if it was safe. They stayed at one displacement camp followed by months in another, where conditions varied depending on the weather. "People helped each other out, but it was muddy," Anouk Noël recalled. Often it didn't feel safe.

Almost a year to the day after the earthquake, Anouk Noël was back home. As part of a program to help the disabled and their families, she and her family received a cash grant. They used it to purchase cosmetic items they resold as a small business venture to provide some income. Their home had also been partially repaired. Anouk sat in a small unfurnished living area, chairs and tables lost in the quake. In one corner of the room stood a wheelchair, given as part of the family's assistance, which Anouk uses when she is out of the house—such as when she sings soprano at regular events for the disabled. Her powerful, commanding singing is a gift, and friends call her a "bundle of joy." But on this day, she was serious and quiet. Living with a physical disability is particularly challenging in a country where mobility is difficult even for the able-bodied. Getting around became even more treacherous in the jagged postearthquake landscape of damaged roads, collapsed buildings, and mounds of rubble.

Rubble. Even a year later, parts of Port-au-Prince lay in rubble. Because on January 12, 2010, in a matter of seconds, Port-au-Prince—the centrifugal force of Haiti, the seat of its government, its economic and social life—had been destroyed, and Haiti had become Rubble Nation.

2

"There Is Still So Much to Do"

In those first days of January it was like this: downtown Port-au-Prince looked as if the quake had happened only hours earlier. Homes and apartments were crushed. The smell of decaying flesh wafted through the air. The sides of some buildings jutted out, looking as if they would fall into the street at any moment. The arbitrary nature of the quake was striking: an untouched building stood next to one that had completely collapsed. It was unsettling to see a building cut in half, with furniture and desks, filing cabinets, and sinks exposed to the harsh midday sunlight. It was even more startling to see those who refused to move to the tent cities. To this day, the worst-hit area of downtown Port-au-Prince remains vivid in my memory because, in the seemingly postapocalyptic rubble and decay, people were angry. They were tired of answering questions from journalists and aid workers. As the sounds of hammers and nails punctuated the air, some shouted at us to go away.

Six months later, it was disheartening to see how little had changed. It was true that parts of Port-au-Prince looked marginally better, as at least some debris had been removed. But generally, the capital city looked beaten down and felt as if it were at a standstill. In some ways a pause was actually needed. Few Haitians I spoke with on July 12, 2010, dwelled on the six-month anniversary of the quake. It was an artificial marker for U.S. journalists and aid workers, who were connected to the outside global media cycle. Haitians were looking only for a break from hardship, misery, and blight. Instead of the anniversary, they focused on the welcome distraction of the World Cup—many people believed that if it were not for the World Cup, the streets of Port-au-Prince would have been filled with protesters, exasperated by the Haitian government's inaction. "People are waiting for someone to show the way to the right place," one of the young Haitian humanitarian workers with the Lutheran World Federation said about the need for leadership and inspiration.

People I spoke to freely acknowledged that the continuing work of repairing, rebuilding, and rehabilitating Haiti had been hindered by endless obstacles and enormous challenges. Haitian aid worker Sheyla Marie Durandisse said, "If you look at the numbers of those we have served, it is impressive. But compared to the continued needs, you see challenge after challenge." Durandisse's colleague, Jean Denis Hilaire, was even more stark in his assessment. "It's like a drop of water in the bucket. There is still so much to do."

At the center of the disappointment and frustration were the hundreds of thousands of people in need of permanent housing who remained stuck in the tent cities. The refrain of "building back better," often repeated after the quake, was heard less and less now that there was actually very little building going on at all. That problem was the result of a number of tangled webs: questions of who owns and who rents land; disputes about whether property owners should be compensated for rubble removal; debates about whether the government could (or should) declare eminent domain and move people out of the crowded camps in Port-au-Prince's public squares, parks, and golf courses. "The biggest challenge that we are facing now is ensuring that everyone has a safe and sustainable place to live," said Prospery Raymond of the UK-based humanitarian agency Christian Aid. "There is not enough land currently available to build permanent houses for everyone who needs them. The Haitian government needs to address that issue as a matter of urgency."

Fueling all of these worries was the perception by many that the Haitian government had not moved quickly enough to resolve these problems. Others argued that neither a weakened government nor well-intentioned nongovernmental organizations—commonly called NGOs—advanced the efforts to assist earthquake survivors. Raymond insisted, "International and local NGOs must improve their level of coordination and collaboration with the state. Now that six months have passed, there is no longer any excuse for not working effectively together."

Long-standing social ills now fully exposed

The fortitude and resilience of Haitians was evident at the St. Thérèse camp in Port-au-Prince. Yvan Chevalier, a member of the camp's management committee, described conditions in his camp of more than 4,300 persons as "stable," but that was the best that could be said. As I watched a group of children kick around a soccer ball for an impromptu game, Chevalier emphasized that any sense of stability would likely be short-lived. "More people are expected here," he said, shaking his head, because another nearby camp was closing down. Life within the camps remained cramped, tense, and uneasy. Residents were still dealing with overwhelmingly crowded conditions, crime, and rape. Downpours, a normal part of Haiti's rainy season, were worsening conditions in the camps. On the day I visited Chevalier's camp, mud was everywhere, despite the brave attempt of residents to build a system of moats and boardwalks to keep water and mud out of the tents. Tent areas were also fortified with stones and concrete to protect against the rains.

Trauma remained an issue—how could it not? "January 12 left us with so many problems," said the Rev. Kerwin Delicat, an Episcopal priest and the principal of the Sainte Croix School in Léogâne, the quake's epicenter. "People are still traumatized," he said. "I see it in the daily life of the people. They are very nervous."

Trauma had done more than simply exacerbate problems that existed in Haiti before the earthquake—misfortunes ranging from poverty to hunger, from overcrowding in Port-au-Prince to poor infrastructure. These long-standing social ills were now fully exposed, as if stripped bare in the devastation of the earthquake. Aaron Tate, one of my Church World Service colleagues, told me that he and others were frustrated by the slow recovery, noting that there "were a lot of dreams early on that this was an opportunity to build a 'new Haiti' better than the old Haiti." But, he said, "the reality is that with such devastation, it is an incredible effort to rebuild at all." Tate said he and others remained firm in their commitment to place the control of rebuilding in the hands of Haitians. But outsiders continually overlooked the reality that the humanitarian workers themselves were still recovering from loss—of loved ones, homes, and jobs. "They are working hard and going far beyond what we could reasonably expect of them to provide emergency relief and recovery, but they do so against great odds," Tate said. While the largest and most critical issues, especially housing in Port-au-Prince, "have been too big for anyone to address," he added, "on a smaller scale, you do see successes."

This was true. While the frustrations and challenges posed in Haiti were most easily witnessed in Port-au-Prince, there was progress around the edges, both in the capital and in other cities affected by the quake. In Jacmel, where house repair was underway, the sense of improvement and energy were palpable. Sainnac St. Fleur, a construction foreman working for Diakonie Katastrofenhilfe, said residents were united in purpose and working hard to see the one-time French colonial city rebuilt. "What we're doing is very important," St. Fleur said. "We have many, many people in need."

It is probably too easy to make facile comparisons between the megalopolis of Port-au-Prince and the smaller, more intimate Jacmel, a less complicated place to work and navigate. Still, judging Haiti solely through the lens of Port-au-Prince might invite pessimism and hopelessness, but I don't think it does. I met too many good, talented, committed, and politically savvy Haitians to believe the naysayers. But it is also obvious that something needed to be done about the scale of congested and crowded Port-au-Prince—the capital is not only too large a spoke in the wheel for all of Haiti, in many respects it's nearly the whole wheel. As St. Fleur, the construction foreman in Jacmel, put it, the capital is not only too big, "it is too politicized a city."

Sylvia Raulo, who was about to leave the Lutheran World Federation to head the Haiti program of Norwegian Church Aid, spoke of the accomplishments of the first six months since the quake this way: given the enormous weight of Haitian history that had produced the problems of malnutrition and hunger, poverty, lack of adequate water and housing, the achievements of the initial six months were perhaps the minimum that could be attained.

She pointed to "the things we haven't heard about. There were no political riots, there was no major food crisis, there was no major outbreak of disease." (This was before the cholera outbreak of late 2010.) "It's an achievement that we've managed to get the horror scenarios out of the picture," she said. "So far, so good." So far. A very cautionary "so far."

But was that good enough? I heard speculation earlier in the year about the need to build new cities outside of Port-au-Prince—visions of a Haitian version of Brasilia, the capital of Brazil which was built in less than four years (1956–1960) in a centralized and "neutral" location, away from Brazil's largest cities. But such talk had abated; unfulfilled visions have a long history in Haiti. *The Comedians*, Graham Greene's satiric novel about Haiti in the mid-1960s, includes a rather somber assessment of the country: "Haiti was a great country for projects. Projects always mean money to the projectors so long as they are not begun."

Should humanitarian agencies criticize governments?

The lack of housing was not the only problem. Relief supplies were held up in customs—not for reasons of malfeasance, but simply because of inefficiencies. Raulo said that humanitarian groups and other nongovernmental organizations had legitimate grievances with the Haitian government in this respect. She told me about a case that demonstrated the obstacles Haitian authorities faced. After Raulo spent a day clearing up a shipment question, she found out that the country's entire customs operation was being run out of an average-size office, no larger than her own, where a dozen harried, overworked employees manage customs for all of Haiti. "There is a real issue of capacity," Raulo said about the losses experienced by the Haitian government—losses that include not only huge numbers of buildings but also equipment and, of course, personnel. "They lost a lot of material and human capital."

Other relief workers were not as diplomatic. Some were publicly impatient—even angry. An op-ed that appeared in the June 25, 2010, *Los Angeles Times* pushed the question of whether or not humanitarian agencies should criticize governments. The author was Erik Johnson, humanitarian response coordinator for the Danish organization DanChurchAid, which works with Christian Aid, Church World Service, and others in an international network of agencies called ACT Alliance. In his piece, Johnson took the Haitian government to task, saying authorities "had lapsed into the classic pattern of corruption, inefficiency, and delay that holds the country hostage." Johnson, a veteran of a number of large-scale emergencies, said that in more than a decade of humanitarian work, he had "never seen camps like those in Port-au-Prince. International standards defining what people are entitled to after a disaster are in no way being met. The Haitian camps are congested beyond imagination, with ramshackle tents standing edge to edge in every square foot of available space." He argued that "massive, aggressive intervention is required" and said the Haitian government had clamped down on the importation of goods, making it difficult for humanitarian assistance to get to beneficiaries. "Though it's important that the Haitian government is in the driver's seat of the recovery effort, it has not yet stepped up to the job," Johnson argued. "The government needs to aggressively facilitate imports of needed goods and equipment and allow agencies to resettle both camp residents who are most at risk and those whose homes were not damaged."

Johnson's piece evoked a number of responses in private. Aid workers within ACT Alliance suggested that Johnson publicly articulated what some observed and said privately—government inefficiencies and roadblocks had hobbled the response in Haiti. But others criticized Johnson, saying it was important that aid groups and humanitarian coalitions not join what one aid worker privately called "the chorus of blanket criticism of government." Of the Haitian government, the worker said, "It is weak, but democratically elected. Strident criticisms from international NGOs will only give succor to even more dubious elements."

Aid workers I spoke to in Haiti in July said that they and their staffs were well aware of the problems, and that some degree of criticism was valid. At the same time, they argued that there is a pragmatic element they have to contend with: Haitian authorities and humanitarian groups would have to find ways to work together in the coming months and years, despite the difficulties they had encountered.

Prospery Raymond of Christian Aid also said that authorities needed to address the issue of any concerns about corruption, a reason often cited for the fact that all but a fraction of the international aid pledged to Haiti by donor governments had not been delivered as of the six-month mark. As of June 2011, only a little more than a third of the $4.6 billion pledged had been given to the government of Haiti. (That aid is separate from the assistance provided by private humanitarian and relief groups, whose assistance had already been used for initial emergency response assistance.) Concurrent with that failure was a concern Erik Johnson expressed about Haiti settling into an old pattern in which elites "continue to live in luxury in elegant homes high above the dusty sprawl" and try to control events to maintain their privilege. Raymond concurred that corruption needed to be investigated, saying Haiti had to move beyond a culture of corruption. "Building back better," Raymond said, "not only means building back better homes, it also means being accountable." He was also adamant that the international community had to deal with the realities of a weakened government that had lost a large number of personnel and much of its own infrastructure, almost two-thirds of its building according to some accounts. Raymond said he wouldn't apologize for insisting that the international community has to find ways to build up and "accompany" the Haitian government. "I think it's good to push the state," he said. "But they still have to get back on their feet."

In one of the numerous stories on the June 12 six-month anniversary of the earthquake, *The New York Times* reported on July 10, 2010, that some of the same complaints about the slow pace of recovery, particularly regarding temporary housing, had been heard in other recent disasters, such as the response to the 2004 Indian Ocean tsunami in Indonesia. "I defy any country on earth to be fully functional at this stage after such a disaster," said Imogen Wall, a spokeswoman for the United Nations Office for the Coordination of

Humanitarian Affairs, quoted by the *Times*. The *Times* story observed that following the 2004 Indian Ocean tsunami, it took the government of Indonesia, which did not suffer anything close to the scale of loss of emergency personnel as Haiti had, more than two years before it was able to move displaced persons out of tent cities.

That was one way of viewing the problem. An ACT representative privately recalled a different attitude expressed by a Haitian colleague at a meeting of humanitarian groups. He said that he was tired of hearing complaints about government inaction. Why? "I do more than the government anyway"—a reference to the fact that many small grassroots groups can often be more nimble and effective than government bodies.

"Things take on a life of their own in Haiti."

"This earthquake was a huge disaster, and we could say, 'We're finished,'" said Ernst Abraham, who heads Service Chretien d'Haiti, a Port-au-Prince–based humanitarian and development agency. "Or we could say, 'Okay, it's a new chance, a new beginning.' If we take the second option, I feel, as a citizen of Haiti, that I cannot go far alone. But then, the world community cannot go alone and cannot go far without the government's help and backup." In other words, humanitarian groups needed Haitian support—both by the government and the public—to be viable. Still, Abraham and others expressed frustration, particularly with the perception that national authorities had discussed reconstruction plans with donor countries—the United States, Canada, members of the European Union—more than with Haitians themselves. More than once, I heard someone say, "We know nothing that is going on," a reference to the low profile, bordering on silence, that President René Préval and his government adopted after the earthquake. (Concerns about the Préval government's response were often cited as why the aid pledged for reconstruction was slow to get to Haiti. Reportedly the United States and others were waiting for a new Haitian government to come to power before much of the reconstruction aid was dispersed.)

For his part, Préval spoke of frustrations about how NGOs were not consulting with his government. As for his initial silence, he apologized, saying, "A president is also only a human being and the worst pain is silent." At the time of the quake he was not at the National Palace, but playing with one of his grandchildren in the garden of his home. "My first reflex was to protect the child with my body," Préval told a radio interviewer, noting that he had a motorcycle taxi driver take him around Port-au-Prince to assess the damage. His response? "I felt defeated and powerless in face of the catastrophe," he said. The *Los Angles Times* reported on August 15, 2010, that Préval is "quiet for a politician, even humble," but that his silence since the disaster enraged many. The president was quoted as saying, "I was much criticized for not having spoken.... To say what? To the thousands of parents whose children were dead. To the hundreds of schoolchildren I was hearing scream, 'Come help me!'... I couldn't find the words to say to those people."

As I drove around Port-au-Prince one evening as residents prepared for another hot, uncomfortable night in tents, it was hard not to feel some of that same sense of defeat and powerlessness. What could anyone say in the face of such massive suffering?

Precious little. Moreover, the pervasive idea that recovery could usher in an invigorated, reborn Haiti had clearly lost some luster. "This 'new beginning' feels like it is proceeding without action to make it real, concrete," Abraham said. "People are losing their faith about this 'new beginning.'"

These frustrations were underscored by a comment made in January by a Latin American humanitarian worker. Speaking of the perceived confidence of outsiders in their ability to manage a massive relief and rehabilitation effort, this colleague—tired and weary from hours of coordination meetings organized by the United Nations—warned of the snares posed by Haiti's complex, politicized realities and history. Noting ruefully that Port-au-Prince felt like it was in the grip "of an occupying force of NGOS," he said Western nations and NGOs "feel like they can come in with their tents, their clusters, and their e-mails, and think they control events. They can't. Things take on a life of their own in Haiti."

They do—with little change for the poor. Survival was still the order of the day for people like Patricia Pierresaint, who lost her husband and daughter in the quake. In July 2010, Pierresaint spent her days as a vendor selling cookies, gum, and sweets at the Place Boyer camp, where she lived in the months after the quake. Her injured legs were still swollen; she received a small monthly stipend from an NGO to assist disabled and injured persons during the difficult first months. Her grant money got her small vending business up and running. Though grateful for the assistance, Pierresaint was eyeing the future with fear. When the six-month stipend ended, what would she do to support herself and her four surviving children? Her small business would not make up for the loss. "You never know what to expect," Pierresaint said about her life in the Place Boyer camp. Women feel threatened by sexual violence, and in such an environment, "I don't have peace of mind." Still, Pierresaint waved off a question about how she felt authorities had responded to the quake and its aftermath. "No, I'm not angry with the government," she said. "It's God's will."

Trying to find cosmic meaning in a disaster

It is impossible to gauge how many people shared Pierresaint's opinion, at least on the theodicy question—of how humans can reconcile the idea of God's love with disasters like Haiti's. Certainly many Haitians tried to find cosmic meaning in the quake. The idea that the disaster was divine retribution for perceived sins in Haitian society was an opinion expressed by many Haitians, particularly those in Pentecostal communities. Others, however, emphatically rejected the idea of divine punishment. The Rev. Kerwin Delicat, the Episcopal priest in the city of Léogâne, said that the disaster "was not a punishment... quite definitely no." Like other church leaders, Delicat was trying to discern how Haitians can find "a way to take responsibility, as human beings, as cocreators with God, to rebuild and reconstruct the country."

That remained a daunting task. Many buildings still posed a hazard as they perched and drooped perilously over hillsides, and numerous tent cities were tattered and falling apart. An area north of Port-au-Prince that had been nothing but deforested hillside in February was now dotted with telltale blue tarps and tents. The devastation I saw in January and February that was almost beyond description seemed almost normal six months later.

In the summer, the downtown area bustled, as if vendors had made their peace with their jagged surroundings. T-shirts and shoes, cookies, and face cream could all be found for sale amid piles of debris. That adaptability seemed to be nothing new for Haitians: the simple task of driving across Port-au-Prince could take ninety minutes—not much more than it did before the quake. More starkly, though, I heard that the logistics of removing all the debris from the country would require at least one thousand trucks working twenty-four hours a day for up to five years.

3

"On the Other Side" of the First Year

On the day I left Haiti after reporting on the one-year anniversary, Jean-Claude "Baby Doc" Duvalier unexpectedly landed at the Port-au-Prince airport. The news was stunning—people had believed that there was a possibility of former President Jean-Bertrand Aristide returning to Haiti, but never Duvalier. Back in New York, I spent the next few days on the phone, tracking down rumors with friends and colleagues in Haiti. The fear expressed by one Haitian friend was palpable, even in an e-mail: memories resurfaced of two of his uncles who had been tortured and imprisoned during the Duvalier years and had emerged from their imprisonment looking like survivors of a death camp. As far away and as distant as the Duvalier years might seem, the fears they evoked could quickly re-emerge.

At first Duvalier's return didn't make sense, but as time went on, it appeared that the former president had gambled that he could come and go from Haiti, proving to European authorities who were trying to claim the last of his ill-gotten fortune that the Haitian government no longer considered him a threat—or an issue. That was one theory, anyway. Of course, in a country of political uncertainty and jarring, startling contrasts and illuminations, nothing is surprising. Still, one reason Duvalier's return felt like such a jolt was because things had been relatively calm in the days before and after the one-year commemorations of the earthquake. Underline that word "relatively"—political violence flared up in December following the first round of presidential elections. Every day during the following month was an occasion for a fresh rumor and worries about contingencies. But, by the time of the second round of elections, in March, violence had cooled—the elections went ahead, and a new president, Michel Martelly, was elected with 60 percent of the vote, though with only a quarter of registered voters casting ballots.

My time in Haiti in January 2011 was less notable for high drama than for more subtle moments. On the morning of the January 12 anniversary, a cortege of Roman Catholic clerics processed onto the grounds of Port-au-Prince's devastated cathedral for a prayer service. One cleric, perhaps recalling the death of Archbishop Joseph Serge Miot in the quake, glanced up and stared hard and wistfully at the ruins of a cathedral whose façade is crumbling, looking like the remains of a structure bombed during World War II.

A headline in a Port-au-Prince newspaper that had appeared prior to the anniversary read: "Just One Day"—as if Haitians wanted just one day of peace, free from outsiders, visitors, missionaries, humanitarian workers, journalists, bad news in general, and the intense (and mostly unflattering) international media glare. Haitian and non-Haitian friends and colleagues told me that most Haitians were likely to just stay home and commemorate January 12 with friends and family. That proved to be true. And in other ways, it seemed that Haitians were relieved to be "on the other side" of the first year. Indeed, during my January 2011 assignment, I felt more keenly the sense of Haitians' eagerness to address long-standing problems and challenges, such as hunger, jobs, and poor governance. Others who had visited Port-au-Prince also saw noticeable change. "I can see a lot of improvements in the city," Henrik Stubkjaer, the general secretary of DanChurch Aid, told me. The tent cities seemed to be better organized—the camps had centralized water and other services. But Stubkjaer also said that he could feel the level of frustration in the camps increasing among the residents. "They've stayed in the camps for a year now and they're fed up. The earthquake has made poverty visible," he said. "The poverty has moved directly into the public parks, the public spaces." The earthquake had simply pushed all of Haiti's long-standing problems—its poverty, its deprivations, its many challenges—out into the streets, for all to see. Haiti's fault lines were visible as never before.

A refocus on Haiti's long-standing problems

Renewed attention to the problems that predated the reappearance of Baby Doc gave way to attention to the baleful legacy he left Haiti. Human rights groups and advocates, for example, condemned Baby Doc's return. In a stinging reminder of what the Duvaliers did to Haiti, author and Haiti expert Amy Wilentz told the Associated Press: "Let's not forget what Duvalierism was: prison camps, torture, arbitrary arrest, extrajudicial killings, persecution of the opposition." Noting that this was not the moment for upheaval in Haiti, Wilentz said, "Haitians need a steady hand to guide them through the earthquake recovery, not the ministrations of a scion of dictatorship."

A refocus on long-standing problems paralleled the sense of normalcy at least physically: As Henrik Stubkjaer noted, Port-au-Prince looked a bit better. In the one year since January 2010, an estimated 8 percent of the rubble had been removed. In the overall scheme of things, that was a small blessing, but it was one notable achievement. The work of Haitian nongovernmental organizations and networks was impressive. From educational and technical training centers in Port-au-Prince, to health clinics and food co-ops in rural areas, these groups are trying their level best to end hurtful dynamics and practices—government inaction and dependence on outsiders—that had done grievous harm to Haiti. Inspired in part by reform movements of the early 1990s that were undergirded by visions of real change, they continued their work, quietly and unheralded. Over the years, they emerged as Haiti's social safety net. Polycarpe Joseph, a Jesuit-trained community leader who heads the Ecumenical Foundation for Peace and Justice, said of his personal vision: "Without social justice, we will not have peace, and without peace, there is not a future for Haiti."

Of course, there is only so much these groups can do; their work filled what could only be described as huge, gaping holes. I asked Josette Pérard, who runs the Port-au-Prince office of the Lambi Fund of Haiti, another small nongovernmental organization, about the greatest threat to Haiti's food security. Without hesitation she replied, "Climate change." That's a problem that obviously requires attention at the international level but also nationally, from a more proactive, robust, and visionary government concerned about Haiti's poor majority—qualities that, to say the least, were not characteristic of Haiti under Baby Doc or his father, Francois "Papa Doc" Duvalier. "The state," Pérard said, "has to take more responsibility."

The state: an absent presence in most people's lives

President Préval did not attend the memorial service for the earthquake victims on the cathedral grounds presumably out of security concerns; the anger people felt over his initial silence remained palpable. Though there had not been any large, singular episode of national chaos since the quake, he was blamed, fairly or unfairly, for just about everything else, including Haiti's new problem: the cholera epidemic. A bit of antigovernment graffiti summed up the frustrations: Préval = Kolera (Cholera).

Préval's decision not to attend the memorial service was probably wise. Despite the apparent calm, anger, even rage, simmered beneath the surface. Not far from the cathedral, a demonstration ended in a Catholic priest's car being torched. The stunned cleric, car keys in hand, stood motionless beside his wrecked vehicle, surrounded by a circle of jostling photographers and reporters. Other demonstrations near the collapsed National Palace—the most potent, painful, and visible symbol of a paralyzed government—were more orderly, but they focused on the widespread weariness, impatience, and anger with Haitian authorities during the past year.

On the afternoon of the one-year anniversary, I went to a mass grave in Titanyen, just outside of Port-au-Prince. It's a striking spot, overlooking the deep turquoise-colored waters of the Gulf of Gonâve. It was a remarkably clear day, though from where we stood, smog still obscured the capital city, which was barely visible against the dominating hills and mountains. But those hills and mountains were beautiful and for a moment, it was possible to see why Haiti was once dubbed "the jewel of the Caribbean." Not many people were at the gravesite, which is set up on a hill and is marked by hundreds of simple black crosses placed where tens of thousands are buried.

Among those at the site was Benjamin Dieufort, one of the drivers who transported truckloads of bodies to the burial grounds in the months immediately after the earthquake.

Dieufort told me that it required 150 trucks over four months to transport the bodies from Port-au-Prince to Titanyen. "I brought a lot of dead here," he said. Among them: his wife's nephew. I asked Dieufort how he had coped during the last year. He said he had experienced nightmares in the early days and weeks, but those had passed. For now, Dieufort was simply happy to be among the living. "It was God," he said, "that gave me the strength to bring the dead here."

4

The Terrible
Weight of Haiti's History

Before Titanyen became the site for burying the quake's dead, it had another notoriety—as the dumping grounds for bodies of political opponents of whatever regime was in power, particularly the Duvaliers. But in the wake of the earthquake and the commemoration of losses a year later, those and other facts were largely ignored or forgotten by the outside world. All that mattered, it seemed, were the events that began on the afternoon of January 12, 2010.

That was a tragic error. Preexisting structural violence, as physician and writer Paul Farmer has noted, is inscribed "into the very seams of Haitian society." Farmer argues: "To foreign eyes, the Haitian story has become a confused skein of tragedies, most of them seen as local…. Poverty, crime, accidents, disease, death—and more often than not their causes—are also seen as problems locally derived. The transnational tale of slavery, debt, and turmoil is lost in Haiti's vivid poverty." That is true. The weight of Haiti's history and its role in the needless death and destruction of January 12, 2010, goes back as far as 1496, when Spain established the first European settlement in the Western Hemisphere on the island of Hispanola, home to both Haiti and the Spanish-speaking Dominican Republic. (In 1697, Spain ceded the western half of Hispaniola to France, and it became Haiti. In Kreyòl, *Ayiti* is a word meaning "high mountains" and derived from the language of the indigenous Taíno peoples, who died with the arrival of the Europeans.)

In time, Haiti was, as author Mark Danner writes, "the world's richest, most productive, and most coveted colony—an enormous slave-powered export factory that produced almost two-thirds of the world's coffee, almost half of its sugar, and large proportions of its cotton, indigo, and cocoa." Thousands of African slaves were brought to the colony to do the backbreaking work of planting and harvesting. Eventually, the ratio of slaves to the white and mulatto ruling class was about ten to one, and slave owners, ever fearful of rebellion, repressed infractions, large and small, with swift and brutal retribution—angry slave owners were known to have disobedient slaves ripped apart by dogs in public or placed in ovens, where they were burned alive.

But the slaves had living memories of Africa, its languages, its religions, and above all else, its freedoms. The slaves only needed a leader for an inevitable rebellion. They found it in former black slave, Toussaint Louverture, who led a slave rebellion and declared himself governor-general. In 1802 he was forced to resign by forces sent by Napoleon Bonaparte to restore French authority in the colony. He was deported to France, where he died in 1803. But the Haitian Revolution continued under his lieutenant, Jean-Jacques Dessalines, who declared Haiti's independence in 1804.

What went wrong after that? While historians do not agree on all points, there is general consensus that the terms of debt France imposed on Haiti after the country achieved its independence—some 150 million francs for, rather incredibly, the loss of its slaves—cost the former colony dearly, putting it on a path toward permanent indebtedness from which it has never recovered. Some historians like Philippe Girard argue that the debt has less to do with Haiti's difficulties than other problems. "Corruption, instability, and xenophobia: these are the main causes of Haiti's decline," he says in his history of Haiti.

Internal tensions in Haiti are certainly real. Some argue there was never any commanding vision for the country beyond the end of slavery, a reality that Danner argues, increased Haiti's "self-absorption and its nationalism, and deepened its internal divisions, cultural and economic, and its suspicion of the colonial powers." Certainly, if there is a consensus among those I met in Haiti—as well as a number of historians—it is that the nation has yet to resolve the vexing issue of a fragmented society. Divisive tensions coexist between a mixed race elite and an overwhelming black racial majority; the language of French spoken by the elite and the Kreyòl spoken by most Haitians; the practice of Christianity and the indigenous religion of Voodoo. Some argue that Haitians can easily unify *against* something but have more difficulty unifying *for* something. One humanitarian aid worker said that Haitians can be warm and welcoming to outsiders but often have "difficulty working well together." Bénédicte Willemart, of the Dutch humanitarian organization ICCO, who is half Haitian and half Belgian, said that while there is trust among family and friends, such trust has been harder to generate in the wider social realm of politics.

Still, the relationship with the outside world has also proved crippling—a fact that can be traced back to the very fact of Haiti's indepedence. In *Damming the Flood*, Peter Hallward argues that there was probably "no single event in the whole of modern history whose implications were more threatening to the dominant global order of things" than the Haitian Revolution. A successful revolt of slaves, defeating the armies of Napoleon, was a "reproach to the slave-trading nations of Europe, a dangerous example to the slave-owning U.S., and an inspiration for successive African and Latin American liberation movements." Much of Haiti's subsequent history, he argues, and its relations to the outside world, have deep echoes in this event, with an "essential legacy of slavery and colonialism" persisting into present times. "Outside Haiti, the slave-owning world immediately closed ranks and locked the island in a state of economic isolation from which it has never recovered."

As an example, France pursued an embargo against its one-time colony until Haiti agreed to pay France the indemnity for its loss of slaves. Haiti was only able to pay this by borrowing from French banks at absurdly high interest rates. Though the amount due France was eventually reduced, the Haitian government was crippled by huge indebtedness throughout the nineteenth century. As the twentieth century approached, Haiti's debts to France still came to more than three-quarters of Haiti's national budget. Meanwhile, France and the U.S. alternately dominated key aspects of the Haitian economy: France had a controlling interest in Haiti's Banque Nationale, which a U.S.-backed consortium took over by 1910.

Haitians, proudly nationalistic, protested these and other indignities, prompting an event rarely recalled in the United States but which echoes to this day in Haiti: the 1915–1934 occupation of the country by U.S. Marines. In *Taking Haiti,* historian Mary Renda said this act was a form of naked domination masked as an act of benevolence, with the United States justifying its role as one of "paternal care and guidance." The occupation was also deeply racist: in the buildup to the U.S. invasion and occupation, William Jennings Bryan, Woodrow Wilson's secretary of state, was incredulous. "Imagine!" he exclaimed. "Niggers speaking French!"

Renda argues that this event was a benchmark in the relations of the first two independent nations of the Western Hemisphere, particularly Haiti: "By crushing Haitian peasant rebellion and by creating the mechanisms for strongly centralized government control in Port-au-Prince, the [U.S.] occupation eliminated the very safeguards against entrenched despotism that Haiti, for all its problems, had always successfully maintained. In doing so, U.S. Americans helped to lay the groundwork for two Duvalier dictatorships and a series of post-Duvalier military regimes."

The Duvaliers' pernicious legacies continue

It is the legacy of those two regimes that still haunts Haiti today—a legacy of fear and murder in the case of the father, and debasement and plunder in the case of the son. "Papa Doc," so named because Francois Duvalier was a physician who had experience in rural areas, was a smart, canny, and wily political leader. He created what Danner called "the intricate dictatorial system that came to be called Duvalierism, and installed himself at its apex, as president for life." A black nationalist who had mixed relations with the United States (and used his estrangements with the United States to his political advantage), Papa Doc based his power partly on his relations with a national network of Voodoo priests, enforced by a secret police known as the Tonton Macoutes. His repressive regime can still cause Haitians of a certain generation to shudder. (It can also, in a time of great uncertainty and loss, elicit nostalgia for a time of perceived order, much as older Russians can feel nostalgia for Stalin. I saw a painting of Papa Doc for sale by an artist peddling his wares at a Port-au-Prince street corner.)

If there was a certain malignant elegance to Papa Doc's style, Jean-Claude Duvalier—who assumed the presidency upon his father's death in 1971—was decadent, careless, sloppy in method, and arrogant in manner. He horrified his father's black nationalist base by marrying a woman of mixed race and, as Danner notes, pulling off such brazen stunts as hosting a televised costume party dressed as a Turkish sultan and handing out expensive jewels as door prizes. Perhaps most damning to his father's old political base—which prized a certain amount of independence from the United States—was Baby Doc's increasing dependence on U.S. assistance. Danner writes that under the son's regime, Haiti was "thrown open. During the first four years of his regime, foreign aid increased tenfold, and it continued to rise sharply. By 1981, when Haiti's entire operating budget had just barely reached $150 million, the country was receiving well over $100 million in foreign aid."

During Baby Doc's reign, Haiti was transformed: the country took up the call from the U.S. and other international lenders to become what one U.S. official called "the Taiwan of the Caribbean"—an export-based economy that would essentially supply the United States and other rich countries with cheap consumer goods. Thousands left impoverished rural areas in hopes of finding work in Port-au-Prince, which saw its slums burgeon.

An appeal based on "telling the truth"

It was from this caldron of despair and hopelessness that Father Jean-Bertrand Aristide emerged. In many ways, he was a figure out of the pages of a Graham Greene novel: a quiet, sometimes uncertain Roman Catholic priest whose appeal, Amy Wilentz noted, often seemed "inexplicable. He is a small, frail-looking person, far from a commanding presence at first sight... ." Yet Aristide's appeal was based on a simple truism—that he spoke "aloud in front of everyone" what the majority of people wanted to say but were afraid to utter in public. "He tells the truth" was a repeated refrain about Aristide.

Well-educated, multilingual, and once called Haiti's best biblical scholar, Aristide was an early and passionate advocate of liberation theology, the theology that emerged originally from Latin America in the 1960s and 1970s, combining elements of spirituality, political activism, and Marxist economic and social analysis. Aristide's writing about the realities of Haiti in the 1980s warned of coming violence; he predicted "one day the people under that table will rise up in righteousness, and knock the table of privilege over, and take what rightfully belongs to them." Such anger was a threat to the military-run governments that ruled Haiti after Baby Doc's departure in 1986, a condition Aristide called "Duvalierism without Duvalier."

It was such clear-eyed passion that, on a wave of hope and a passionate victory for the "Lavalas" movement that he championed, Aristide was elected president in 1991. He represented a movement based in the "popular church" that had urged him to run. Soon, though, Aristide, once seen as unconquerable, was, as Wilentz argues, ultimately "brought down by the hard facts of Haiti." He was subsequently ousted in a September 1991 coup; returned to power in 1994 with U.S. support, though under terms that critics felt tied his hands. He won the 2000 presidential election, serving as president from 2001 to 2004, until he left the country in what remains a contested version of events: the Bush administration says he left voluntarily in the face of chaos and threats to his own safety; Aristide claims he was, in effect, put on a plane by the United States and summarily flown off to exile in Africa.

In his exhaustive study of Haiti's history from 1991 onward, Peter Hallward mounts a point-by-point argument that Aristide was the victim of a deliberate disinformation campaign. Hallward argues that far from being a firebrand in office, Aristide was actually pragmatic to a fault, trying to run a government that "was already verging on bankruptcy. Its social and economic programs were already compromised by concessions extorted by the U.S., the IMF [International Monetary Fund], and the domestic elite." (Haitians have called such neoliberal reforms "the death plan.")

Aristide himself was aware of the dilemmas any Haitian government would face: the realities of a domestic elite that did not want change, the immense power and weight of the United States and its lending institutions, and the pressures of globalization. The dilemma, Aristide argued, was the classic dilemma facing the poor: the choice "between death and death." He said: "Either we enter a global economic system, in which we cannot survive, or we refuse, and we face death by slow starvation." Moreover, Aristide warned: "If the international community is not for us, one thing is sure: we will fail."

Toppled by corruption or by outside forces?

To his critics, Aristide did fail—becoming erratic, autocratic, and out of touch with his populist roots, they claim. On a play of his well-known nickname, Titid, historian Philippe Girard labeled him "Boss Titid." Others were even less charitable, saying that Aristide had become as corrupt and authoritarian as any of his predecessors. Among the charges leveled against the Aristide government was its alleged involvement in the illegal drug trade, a ham-fisted approach toward governing, and even, some say, interference with humanitarian groups working in the country. While time has eased some of that anger, several of my Haitian humanitarian colleagues—including some who knew Aristide before he became president—feel he went down the wrong path in entering politics. "That's not the man I used to know," Polycarpe Joseph, who studied under Aristide, recalled after a 1992 meeting. "He had changed." Herode Guillomettre, a Haitian Protestant leader who heads the Christian Center for Integrated Development, a church-based humanitarian agency, acknowledges Aristide's place in history: "He was the first Haitian to really make an international impact." But Guillomettre faults Aristide for not unifying the nation. "He became a symbol of Haiti's divisions," Guillomettre said. It is true that Haiti's poor and illiterate make up Haiti's majority, and they were the cornerstone of Aristide's base, he notes. "But you can't develop a country with just them," Guillomettre said. "You need all sectors; you need to create a bridge between all people."

Still, it has to be acknowledged that affection for Aristide is still real in many quarters. Pierre Saint Fritz Robert, an unemployed car washer who lives in a tent on a hardscrabble corner of downtown Port-au-Prince in the shadow of the destroyed National Cathedral, told me on Easter Day 2011 that Michel Martelly, the eventual winner of the 2011 presidential elections, reminded him a bit of Aristide, whose professed return from an African exile to promote educational efforts in Haiti has been greeted warmly by many. The comparisons between the two men are not political—in fact, Martelly has been an Aristide critic and has been called a "neo-Duvalierist" for past friendships with political figures on the right, including some accused of human rights abuses. Rather, the comparisons are in style: Martelly was the only candidate who had visited Robert and his neighbors and had promised to do his best to improve their lives, something that reminded Robert of the former president. "Aristide was always thinking of the poor people," he said. "I'm not sure why he came back and why he came back now, but if he builds some schools and helps those in need, that would be good." Robert paused and repeated a thought. "He was always thinking of the poor people."

Aristide's continued popularity extended to an ally, Rene Préval, who was elected president in a disputed 2006 election. Even those unhappy with his postquake leadership have acknowledged that Préval's prequake leadership wasn't bad: under his helm, Haiti experienced some political reform, made a bit of progress in attracting foreign investment, and was relatively calm and stable. That stability collapsed on the afternoon of January 12, 2010, a reminder of what former President Leslie Manigat had once said about moments of crisis in Haiti: that they were events of "conjuncture"— "a moment of nudity, propitious for applying the stethoscope to the social body." When the rubble began to fall, it was clear that the unresolved legacies of the Duvialier and Aristide years—of, respectively, corruption and still-born dreams of reform and change—still haunted Haiti.

5

In the Camps and on the Streets: The Quest for Dignity

The issue of politics quickly came into play when Garry Auguste, a young Haitian teacher who worked as a translator, showed me around one of the displacement camps during the first weeks following the quake. While he predicted that Haiti would see better days, such optimism was tempered by his own difficulties: the school where he taught had been destroyed and he did not expect it to reopen; he knew a number of people who had perished, including two of the pastors of his Pentecostal church. Yet he did not dwell on his own problems; rather, he repeated what would become a mantra in the coming weeks and months: the Haitian government could not be trusted—it was too corrupt and incompetent. "Haitians are a very dynamic people and do not ask for much from the government," he said. "Just a minimum." But even the minimum was out of reach. "The problem is that government uses its power in the wrong way."

"It's the same heads," he said—a cycle of revolving personalities who fit a single profile: upper class, with families living in the United States, Canada, or France. "The only connection the elite have to average people is during the election, when they give out food to voters. But then the same business-as-usual starts up again." That was likely to be played out in a scenario in which people might live in camps for up to three years. (If anything, that might be understating the case.) Part of that problem, he said, would be based on unresolved land title issues that plague the country. "When it comes to land, people fight a lot," he said.

The camp we visited was in the Port-au-Prince suburb of Pétionville and had once been a country club golf course. It would receive its lion's share of media attention in the coming months as the camp where actor and humanitarian Sean Penn ran a well-respected aid operation. It was teeming with people, and though thousands struggled with injuries, hunger, and loss, life appeared fairly orderly. Charilien Charles, a barber, had reestablished his business in the camp. He had retrieved the mirror and supplies from his damaged shop and was able to attract both old and new customers. But the number of clients in the camp fell far short of what it had been—perhaps one for every thirty who had visited before. "It's unpredictable," he said. Saint Elene Alcidonis, a mother of seven children, ages ten to twenty-four, was newly widowed. Alcidonis's late husband, Jean-Claude Bien-Aime, a mason and carpenter who perished in the quake, was the family's principal breadwinner. Alcidonis's immediate needs were taken care of—she had been provided with food, water, and a tent. But her long-term worry was what would happen six months, a year, five years later. Without a home to return to and the loss of her husband's income, she feared for her family's future. "It could be months, I don't know what to expect," Alcidonis told me as she prepared the family's strong morning coffee. "There are so many to take care of," she said about her large family. The best she could hope for? School would reopen for her younger children and her older children could work to support the family. She expressed some optimism. "Yes, in the name of Jesus, I believe it will happen."

This capacity to embrace some kind of normalcy was, at times, quietly moving. A week after visiting that camp, Auguste and I found ourselves in Port-au-Prince's downtown area, among the worst-hit areas from the quake. He recalled January 12 and described a few things he saw and experienced that day. He was outside, and as the street buckled under him, he saw people crushed, "broken legs, torn legs, exposed bones." He fell silent. As we navigated around some muddy streets, we could smell the stench of decaying flesh. I saw an older woman in her Sunday hat and high heels, using her cane to navigate the mud and muck of what had once been a sidewalk. Auguste noticed the woman. While the Haitian people lived in seeming chaos right now, he said, they were doing their best to cope amid what we called "this disunity"—the indignities, terrors, and flashbacks; the chaos, mud, and muck.

Disunity, uncertainty, coping—all became watchwords

Uncertainty haunted Haitians as they traveled the unknown in a shattered and unwelcoming world. The immediate future—a day, a week—could only be guessed at. As a result, people feared staying in a house or building because it might collapse; they picked their way through and around piles of rubble; they suffered the embarrassment of conducting private acts in public. All of this had become part of daily life. Such indignities caused anger and upset. Some of the many impromptu signs not only declared, "We're hungry," but also "We're angry." Some Haitians believed that the trauma that would be felt by many as time went on might lead to violence. For women, violence was not some future threat: reports of rape at displacement sites were becoming increasingly common, and they continued unabated for the next year. Women were wearing as many as four pairs of jeans as protection against the threat of rape. Mirasol Baez, who works with the Movement of Dominican-Haitian Women, a local NGO responding to the needs of women in the camps in Léogâne, said women were "afraid to talk, as the perpetrators often live by their side in the camps and they felt threatened that if they speak they could lose their life." Whistles and flashlights had been distributed to her group; that had done some good, but that was not all that was needed.

In an interview with the NGO, an eighty-five-year-old rape survivor said she did not want to recount the crime—"talking about it will bring it back and I don't want to bring it back"—though she did say that she was "already in bad shape so obviously I was worse after that. And because it was so early after the quake, the earth was still shaking, we were in total confusion, there was no doctor anywhere, and I stayed lying there for days." When she was asked about a sense of safety for herself and others, the survivor said, "Security starts with safe housing. As long as we live under tarps and tents, I don't think we can find security." Haiti, she said, was now a ruined, decimated country, and she was not optimistic about its future. "What can I tell you: the only thing that would help is to have a job and have some money. As least we could eat everyday. At the moment we eat when we eat, day by day."

Will I ever again be able to say "I'm home?"

To understand the overall frustration, it helps to understand the context. When people's homes came crashing down, survivors lost not only family members, friends, and most material possessions, but also their sense of security. In its place came terrifying questions: Will I ever have a home again? Do I dare send my child back into a still-standing school building? When—if ever—can I return to work? Will there be work? What do I do for a living—to feed the family right now—and in ten months time? How will we find proper shelter during the rainy season? Will I ever again be able to close a door behind me and say, "I'm home?"

People were fond of saying that Haitian society "had a lot of coping mechanisms"—and no doubt that was true. Non-Haitian NGO workers repeatedly described Haitians as resilient. True enough—though those statements, while well-meaning, also began to sound almost patronizing when repeated constantly. And such comments did not take into account the extent of trauma in people's lives: adults usually bore the deepest psychological scars; children seemed to recover more quickly if their families survived. "If the mother and father are there, they can cope," said Bjorg Roedland, a Norwegian nurse. "But if the parents are missing, it's much more difficult for the children." It was true that programs to assist children were generally easier to organize: I spent an afternoon with some children at a displacement camp in the Belair neighborhood of Port-au-Prince. For years before the earthquake, it was widely considered one of Port-au-Prince's most dangerous areas. By many accounts, the gang mediation efforts of a Brazilian NGO, Viva Rio, helped to reduce violence considerably in the months prior to the quake. For a few months anyway, the camp—enclosed in the Viva Rio compound—was a place where survivors like the children I met could at least find a minimum semblance of normality. One of the psychosocial programs for children involved the practice of *capoeira*, an Afro-Brazilian martial art taught by Viva Rio staff and used as therapy for young people recovering from trauma. Drawing was another form of trauma therapy.

The five children I spoke to, ages seven to ten, spoke about their lives with a poignant mixture of sadness and optimism. Though none lost immediate family, all understood the immensity of the earthquake. "Too many people died in our country," said Mario Pierre, one of the children. That sense of enormity had clearly affected ten-year-old Nacilien Josue. When I asked him what he wanted to do when he grew up, he replied, "Become a ship captain to bring in medical supplies."

Later, I spoke to Marie Sylsalve, a young mother who cradled her ten-day-old son, McAnley. Sylsalve had last seen her husband, Andre, in the moments immediately following the earthquake. She saw a wall fall on Andre and presumed he was dead; she had not seen or heard from him in the intervening days. "He was very hurt," she said. "He probably died." Twelve days later, she gave birth to McAnley, her fourth child. His birth cheered her somewhat. But Sylsalve, who used to work as a vendor, was now faced with the problem of supporting her infant son and three other children. She had no immediate prospects for work. She retained some hope for her infant, saying that "everything that comes his way will be good." She spoke tersely and dispassionately, continuing to cradle McAnley. When I returned to Haiti in mid-2010, I asked about Sylsalve. The camp where she stayed had been shut down. Eventually, Viva Rio had to reclaim its work space—and there was no immediate word about her whereabouts.

The camps: the most visible example of the horror

In one sense, the closure of the camp struck me as indescribably sad—I didn't like the idea of Sylsalve and her children wandering the streets and looking for a place to live. But I also knew the camps were, at best, places of fragility that could never be called home. They were the most visible examples of Haiti's postdisaster horror. One day my colleagues and I stopped at a newly formed "tent city" and it was hard to tell who was actually running the camp. Community leader Altenor Ronald confessed that he was dazed, angry, and anxious about a host of things—the effects of the quake, the fact that no aid was forthcoming, and that basics like food were not available. Somehow, though, the community had found tarps and tents to provide some shelter. "We have no food, no stoves, people are hungry," he said, nearly choking and crying. "I'm in charge and I don't know what to do." Eventually he told me that his neighborhood near Port-au-Prince was in a pocket where, he claimed, no aid groups were present. Given frustrations over that and lingering concerns about the safety of the buildings, he and his neighbors decided that their only option was to relocate. He said that people were so desperate, hungry, and sick that in one case, a mother felt compelled to urinate in a pot and give the liquid to a thirsty child. He pleaded, "Please make our request known so that the world understands our problems." One of the camp residents who was trying to organize an orderly placement of tents, Elimeme Jean, said she and others worried that they would have to leave within two months. But six months later, it looked as if the camp had expanded considerably, perhaps even doubled in size. By January 2011, it looked even larger. It had become a small suburb.

Haitians and the quest for dignity

Dignity and pride mean a lot to Haitians—Aristide even wrote a book with the title *Dignity*—and it was a theme at the center of several conversations I had with Prospery Raymond. When I first met Raymond in Port-au-Prince, the Haitian country manager of the British-based humanitarian organization Christian Aid was not only coordinating the response to the disaster but also finding new quarters. His agency's offices collapsed during the quake, and he was among those trapped for a time under the rubble. Astrid Nissen, the German humanitarian worker, recalls a frantic Raymond—covered in white dust and nursing a leg wound—coming to her office on the night of January 12 to use a computer to alert his London colleagues to what had happened. Like thousands of other Haitians, Raymond initially had a tough time keeping mind and body together because of trauma. "I do not have words to describe what I have seen in the street, I have never seen so many dead bodies," he told colleagues at the time. Raymond was a realist, but his greatest asset was also, in the midst of such hardship, being able to find strength and positivity amid the turmoil. "I'm optimistic," he said. "Yes, this happened, but it has to be seen as an opportunity to rebuild the country."

From the first moment I met Raymond, he stressed that while Haitians deeply appreciated the international response to the earthquake, the relief agencies had to respect the dignity of Haitians. For him, dignity was not just a watchword: whatever happened in Haiti had to be *with* Haitians and not merely *for* Haitians. "If Haitians themselves are not involved in reconstruction efforts, it could be a waste of time and money," he said. "It would not be wise." It would not be wise for a host of reasons—not the least of which was the extreme weight of history and the fraught legacy of Haiti's relations with outside powers like France and the United States. But the most obvious reason, he argued, is that Haitians know their local circumstances and conditions better than outsiders.

During the early months of 2010, that simple truth was often overlooked. In a 2010 report, Refugees International criticized the lack of coordination between the UN and local Haitian groups. "The first step to improving humanitarian programs in Haiti is for the UN and international agencies to link into Haiti's civil society network," the report said. "There is a strong, organized civil society comprised of grassroots community-based organizations under umbrella networks."

The dynamic of Haitians helping other Haitians

Overlooked also, in the rush of stories, images, and narratives of international aid workers in Haiti, were the numerous informal and local Haitian relief and self-help efforts. Most noticeable of these endeavors is that an estimated 600,000 people from Port-au-Prince fled to the countryside after the earthquake and survived thanks to the solidarity of family and friends in small, impoverished rural towns and villages. One of those doing so was Fontil Louiner, a thirty-nine-year-old video technician who, faced with the reality of damaged homes and lost income, fled Port-au-Prince with more than two dozen family members and friends. They returned to his hometown of Petite Rivière, in the northern department (province) of Artibonite, which was not hit by the quake, and made it a popular destination of return—an estimated 162,500 arrived there after the quake.

Louiner was no stranger returning home to Petite Rivière. While Louiner worked in Port-au-Prince for twenty years, he maintained his ties with his hometown by serving, since 2004, as a part-time manager and DJ of a local radio station, Family Radio. The station is committed not only to broadcasting music, but also to providing a public service function, airing news and educational programming. That is no small role. In Haiti, radio is a significant social player—some call it the "engine of society." Family Radio has ties with a consortium of Haitian community-based agencies that, in turn, have relationships with Haitian and U.S. church groups. Together, these groups responded to floods in the region in the years before the earthquake.

So it made sense for the station to galvanize support for a grassroots-run meals program. Working with the Haitian Council of Non-State Actors (CONHANE), one of the community-based agencies, and RTA, another radio station, Family Radio broadcasted an appeal for food and cash donations. One of the appeals was simple: "If you have a family of six people, please donate a goblet of rice." The effort paid off, at least initially, with local residents dropping off rice, other foods, and cash donations to provide 500 meals daily for the displaced Port-au-Prince residents, many of whom have ties to the region. Station employees and volunteers prepared the meals at a feeding center adjacent to the Family Radio offices and studio. "We know they need these meals," Louiner told me, but added that among all—employees, volunteers, and recipients—"there is a lot of sharing." Louiner and his Family Radio colleagues knew this was far from a permanent solution to the displacement issue. What the future might hold for the displaced—who were staying in family homes, in tents, and public spaces like schools—was still not clear.

"Nobody knows how long we'll be here," Louiner said of the displaced people. "But we do know it's not possible to go back to Port-au-Prince." He downplayed any possible tensions between the new arrivals and the community, saying the arrivals had been warmly welcomed. "They've become naturalized citizens here," he told me, a feeling he and other family members have experienced as well. "We're very proud to be back here."

Trying to stay together as a community

Another example of Haiti's indigenous self-help activities is in the experience of the southern coastal city of Jacmel. Like Port-au-Prince (and unlike Petite Rivière), Jacmel was severely affected by the quake. But their efforts to recover from the disaster did not receive the same level of attention as those of the capital. Gerald Mathurin, director of the Haitian nongovernmental organization KROSE—in its English translation, Coordination of Organizations in the South East Region—emphasized his agency's commitment to "localized" humanitarian efforts. With some initial support and encouragement from KROSE, a sense of dignity was kept alive for those who wished to stay together as a community and did not want to move into displacement camps. Among "Groupes Solidarités," or informal solidarity groups, friends and neighbors decided to stay together, even on borrowed land, and in conditions that were noticeably more exposed than those of the camps. But it gave the solidarity groups access to their homes, which had been either damaged or destroyed.

The numbers were not small. There are typically between 50 and 200 people in the solidarity groups, and in Jacmel alone there are more than 400, representing an estimated total of some 31,505 persons. "There are some people who want to see their house everyday," said Francilaire Jeudi, a young leader of a solidarity group staying in and around the grounds of Jacmel's Wesleyan (Methodist) Church, which received assistance from KROSE and the World Food Program. "Even if you can't go into it, you want to see it." He conceded their stay on the church grounds could be months, perhaps even longer. "How long will it be? I don't know," said community leader Francilaire Jeudi. "Nobody knows." Still, the members of this solidarity group were determined to remain together within the city rather than relocate to a displacement site on Jacmel's outskirts. "This place is better than the camp because here we can organize ourselves," said Thifaut Jean, another community leader. Other reasons cited: a sense of security, unity, and belonging. "Here," said Francilaire Jeudi, "we're one family."

Did these efforts succeed? In mid-2010, the meals program had been cut back, understandably, because only a portion of those who fled from Port-au-Prince remained in Petite Rivière. Many had returned to the capital for practical reasons: humanitarian aid such as cash-for-work programs was easier to access; numerous family members had remained there; and, most tellingly, there were no long-term jobs and few good schools to be found in Petite Rivière.

The situation in Jacmel was more complicated. While the solidarity groups struck a chord of idealism, it was also clear that this would be hard going—the tarps and canvas being used on the grounds of the Methodist Church were already tattered and ragged. Compared to the more formally organized displacement camps that ringed Jacmel, where rows of tents had been established in an orderly fashion, the site of the solidarity group at Jacmel looked in bad shape.

When I saw the area later in 2010, the church grounds looked neater and more orderly. Classes were being held in a school tent. Sturdier tents had been provided by Jacmel authorities to replace the older, worn-out ones. Still, much remained unsettled. Francilaire Jeudi, the community leader I had spoken to in January, said that the numbers of people staying at the site had dropped from 400 to 150. Some decided they would rather go it alone and returned to their homes or went to other areas. As is often the case during relief operations, food assistance provided in the initial emergency phase had ended. "It's been hard to keep up," Jeudi said about the solidarity group. Later I learned from a Canadian news report that the community had splintered into different factions: some from the splinter group were unhappy with leadership. They eventually left the church grounds and moved down the street at another site. Jeudi stressed that the school classes were for the wider community and that fifteen children from the solidarity group living on the church grounds were attending classes. Long-term concerns remained, including worries about food and the need for jobs. Some in the solidarity group had received cash-for-work assistance, but others had not and were barely getting by. Jeudi was among those still looking for a job. "I have to work," he said. As of mid-2010, he still had no immediate prospects.

6

The Reinvasion of the "Republic of NGOs"

The night before I left on my first assignment to Haiti in January 2010, Martin Coria, a Church World Service colleague from Argentina, warned me that the scale of the disaster was beyond anything he had ever seen. "The magnitude of this makes you feel useless. The destruction was beyond comprehension," he said of his first weeks in Haiti. "It is *beyond* comprehension." Coria found some hope in the fact that the first responders to the quake had been from the Dominican Republic, and that the quake might help lower long-standing tensions and uneasy relations between the neighboring countries. "It's humane, in the best sense, to love your neighbor. Haiti needs the Dominican Republic and the Dominican Republic needs Haiti," he said. Almost as quickly, he made a prediction that the earthquake would push aid agencies to end the notion that they were the response.

Coria lamented that there had always been a "fixer mentality" about Haiti, as if each single-issue component of what aid agencies had done through the years—dealing with problems like malnutrition, finance, and literacy individually—was by itself the solution. That led to expectations that humanitarian agencies could, by themselves, "fix things that are broken." In order to be effective, he insisted that aid agencies would have to explain that what they do is actually a small part of a larger effort—an effort that could take a decade or more and would require staying power and close collaboration with Haitian agencies. Humanitarian relief agencies would have to tell their donors that the efforts in Haiti would require attention, time, and patience. "There are no miracle approaches," he said. And by the way, he said, "Port-au-Prince looks like it's been invaded by an army."

He was right. It *did* appear that way, and we—the employees of aid agencies—were the invaders. NGO vehicles were everywhere: here was World Vision, there was the UN, over there were mom-and-pop operations, many of them run by U.S. evangelical

A "SUPER" girl in the Haitian village
of Foret des Pins.

TWO GIRLS WALK to school in the Haitian village of Foret des Pins, high in the mountains east of Port-au-Prince.

FARMERS HARVEST cabbages (below) in the mountainous community of Foret des Pins.
Behind them is a hillside where trees have been planted as part of a reforestation project.
Plagued by deforestation—much of it to produce charcoal for urban cooking stoves—
residents of this community are working with advisors from the Lutheran World Federation
to reforest and protect their environment. In the above image, nineteen-year-old Joselin
Jerome works in a field in the same village.

FARMERS WORKING in their fields in Foret des Pines. Agriculture in Haiti has been handicapped by government centralization, the lack of land reform, and the removal of tariffs on imported commodities such as rice.

RURAL HAITIANS LOAD A TRUCK with sacks of charcoal (above) they have produced from trees in the mountainous community of Foret des Pins. The charcoal is trucked to the capital, where it is used by poor families for cooking. Charcoal production is one of the main causes of deforestation in Haiti. Nicole Phitrion (below), a member of Haitian Artisans for Peace International in the remote village of Mizak, is trying to change that. The group provides income-generating opportunities for poor rural residents, and she has leveraged her income from artisan work into a variety of home-based businesses, including making bread in a solar oven, which doesn't consume firewood.

CHABINE PHITRION COOKS over a fire (above) in the Haitian village of
Belande, while two women (below) walk along a rural road in Foret des Pins.

THE UNITED STATES MILITARY is never far away from Haiti. In 2004, after democratically elected President Jean Bertrand Aristide was overthrown by the U.S., Leon Charles (above) was named chief of police. Here he speaks with police officials in a private meeting in the northern city of Cap Haitien. Behind him are officials of the U.S. Marines (left) and U.S. Navy (right) who refused to be identified. During the same year, U.S. Marines (below) patrol the streets of Port-au-Prince.

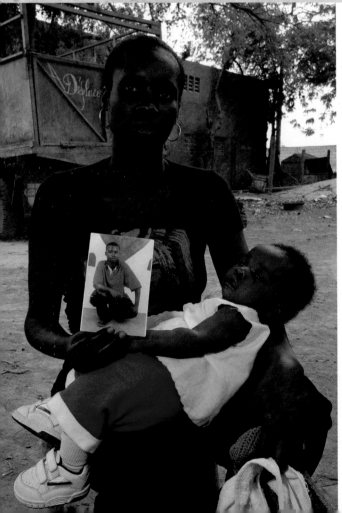

AN INDIAN SOLDIER (above), part of the giant United Nations Mission in Haiti (MINUSTAH), which some consider a form of military occupation. MINUSTAH's presence didn't help Yrena Clervoyant's husband, Joseph, who was killed in the fighting that broke out in 2004 after President Jean Bertrand Aristide was overthrown. Clervoyant (below) holds her three-month-old daughter, Walkins.

PROTESTORS RALLY outside a Catholic Mass in Port-au-Prince that marked the one-year anniversary of the January 12, 2010, earthquake that devastated Haiti. The demonstrators, who burned a priest's car, were upset about the government's management of the quake recovery. At the Mass, Jean Pirame yells in an attempt to interrupt the service, shouting that President Rene Préval should resign and the country should bring back former President Jean Bertrand Aristide. Aristide returned to Haiti less than three months later, saying he would concentrate his energies on educational reform.

FIREFIGHTERS EXTINGUISH A FIRE in a car outside a Catholic Mass in Port-au-Prince that marked the one-year anniversary of the January 12, 2010, earthquake that devastated Haiti. The car, which belonged to Father Allan Francois, was set afire by protestors upset about the government's management of the quake recovery. Violence also broke out at several times during an electoral campaign in late 2010 and early 2011, though inside Marie Carmel Telisme's tent in a camp in Grand-Goave, competing candidates coexist peacefully as they provide decoration. Telisme, who is accompanied by her son Myson Merville, was left homeless by the 2010 earthquake.

A NURSE CHECKS a pregnant woman (above) in a church-run hospital in Pere Payen, part of a church-supported program. Much of the health-care system in Haiti is run by private groups because the Haitian elite have never been very interested in providing services to the poor. One of the outside groups that has provided considerable resources is the Cuban government. Magdalena Mauri Gomez (below) is one of more than five hundred Cuban health-care professionals who were serving in Haiti before the quake. Gomez is a nurse, and the boy and his mother are suffering from a variety of malnutrition-caused ailments.

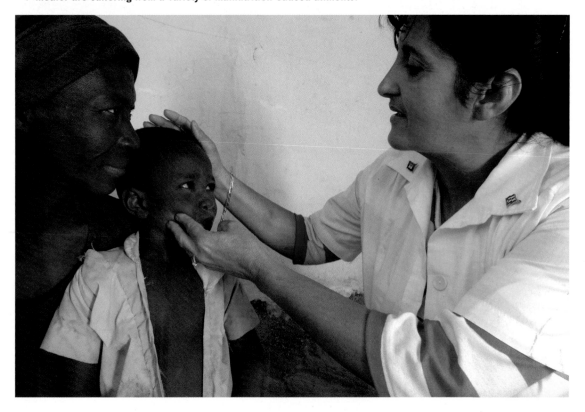

IN THE HEAT OF PORT-AU-PRINCE, a man (above) carries medicines to sell in the Croix-des-Bossales market in the La Saline neighborhood. Health care faces many obstacles, including the bleak poverty of a girl (below, left) who crawls in the dirt in Cité Soleil, a poor neighborhood of Port-au-Prince. The poor often have difficulty gaining access to clean and safe water, though eight-year-old Caitland Dirocher (below, right) found some to carry home to her family, who is living in a tent camp for families left homeless from Haiti's 2010 earthquake. The camp, in the Martissant section of Port-au-Prince, houses hundreds of displaced families who are receiving medical care and other services from Dominican solidarity groups.

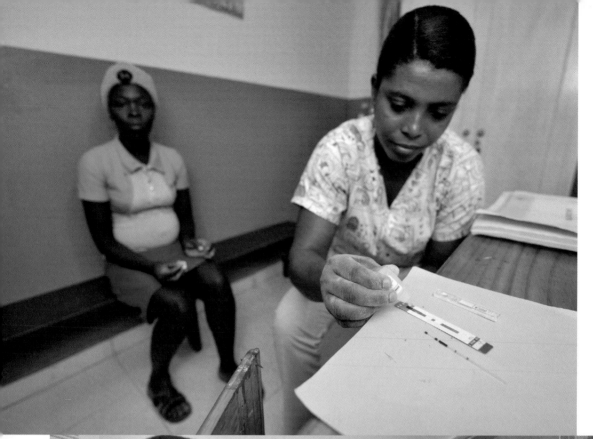

HIV AND AIDS have had a huge impact on Haitians. Here are three aspects of an HIV and AIDS program run by the St. Boniface Hospital in remote Fond des Blancs. Christela Pierre (on page 44, above) watches while nurse Joseph Marie Lernise processes her rapid test for HIV. Pharmacist Jean Darcelin (on page 44, below) explains the dosage on antiretroviral medication to Matilde Meleus, who is living with HIV. Her six-year-old daughter Ketia looks on. And on this page (above), Marie Carline Leopold (right), the ARV coordinator at the St. Boniface Hospital, visits Cledanie Joseph in her home. Joseph also lives with HIV, and the hospital conducts an aggressive outreach program to service their needs and combat stigma and discrimination in the community. On this page (below), a patient sits on her bed at the "House for the Dying," a hospice for AIDS patients and other terminally ill patients run by the Sisters of Charity in Port-au-Prince.

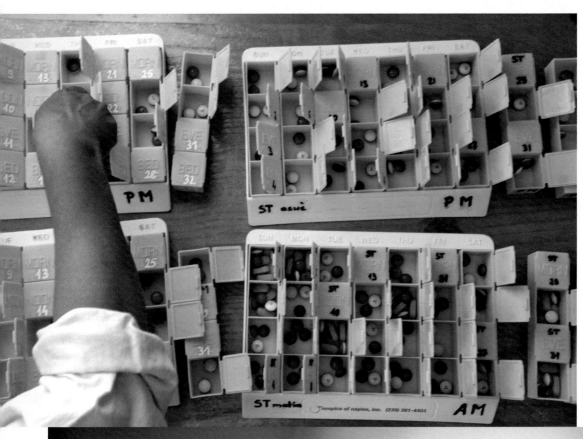

MEDICINES, INCLUDING antiretroviral drugs, get sorted (on page 46, above) into individual boxes before being administered to patients living in the "House for the Dying." On page 46 (below), a patient at the House lives on faith and medication. On this page (above), a patient passes the day. Also on this page (below), Sister Paula, a Spanish nun, supports a patient as she walks.

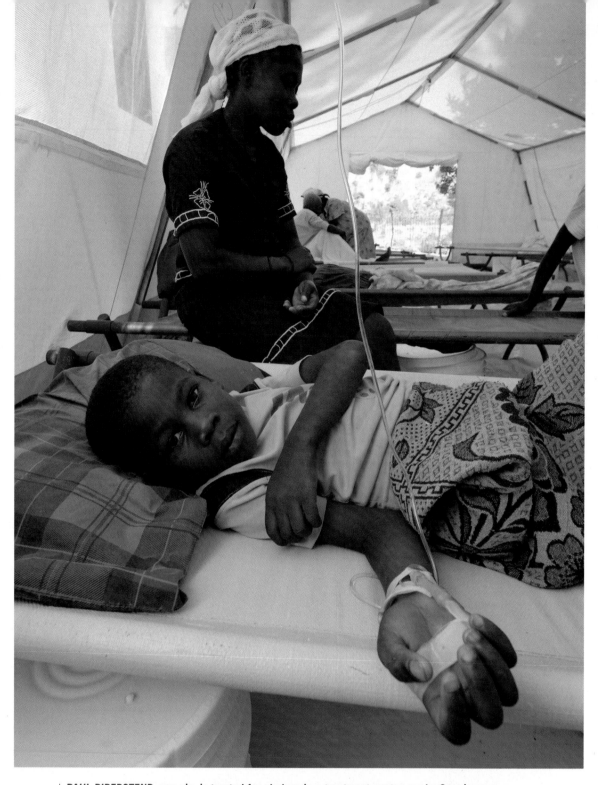

PAUL BIBERSTEND, age six, is treated for cholera in a treatment center run by Oganizasyon Sante Popile (OSAPO) in Montrouis. With him is his mother, Odette. Cholera appeared on the quake-ravaged Caribbean island nation in late 2010. OSAPO's work is supported by the ACT Alliance. In addition to treating people infected with cholera, OSAPO sends teams of health educators into urban and rural communities to provide education, distribute antibacterial soap and oral rehydration salts, and refer sick patients back to the OSAPO clinic.

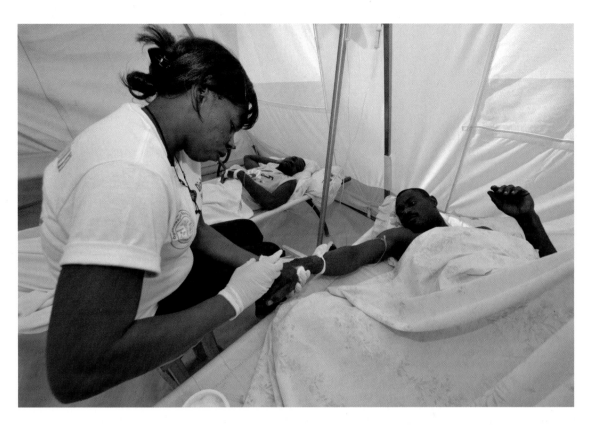

AIME MINOUCHE (above), a nurse for OSAPO, puts an intravenous needle into the hand of Prenelus Brimel, a patient with cholera being treated in a special OSAPO cholera clinic in Montrouis. In the below image, Sonia Noel mops the floor of the cholera clinic.

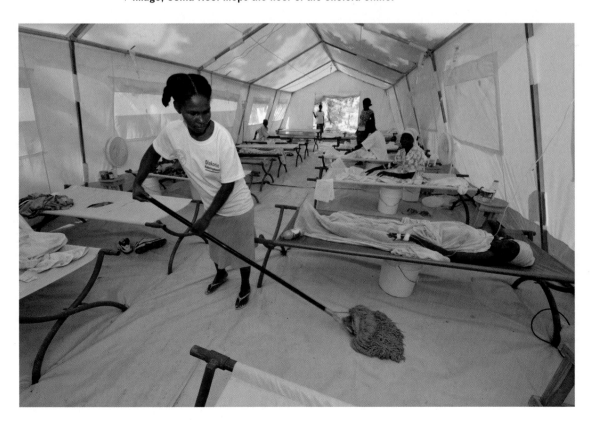

COMBATTING CHOLERA MEANS EDUCATION. In the above left image: Haitian girls learn proper hand-washing techniques, including the use of antibacterial foam, during activities at a youth center run by the YWCA in Petionville. In the above right image: A girl gets help from health workers to wash her hands after using the toilet in Cité Soleil, a poor neighborhood of Port-au-Prince. In the below image: Isma Alexis (with megaphone), a community health worker for OSAPO, speaks in the town market to residents of Montrouis about steps they can take to prevent the spread of cholera. Health workers from OSAPO go out to surrounding neighborhoods and communities, providing education, distributing antibacterial soap and oral rehydration salts, and referring ill patients to the group's clinic.

AT THE "HOUSE FOR THE DYING," Guerto Toussaint enjoys a package of Plumpy'nut, a high protein and high energy peanut-based paste that is used as a ready-to-use therapeutic food. The boy suffers from glandular tuberculosis.

FORDING A STREAM, a boy walks home from school in the remote
Haitian village of Embouchure.

IN THE ABOVE IMAGE, RENAUD JEROME, waters seedlings in a nursery that's part of a reforestation project in the mountainous community of Foret des Pins. Jerome and other residents are producing seedlings for transplanting onto nearby mountainsides. In the below image, residents of the village of Mizak carrying plants to a reforestation project.

KENTIA JEROME, twelve, holds seedlings grown for Foret des Pins'
reforestation projects.

IN THE ABOVE IMAGE, NOVEMBRE SIMON, carries a small pine tree for replanting as part of a reforestation project in the rural village of Foret des Pins. Yet urban residents are also working to improve the environment. In the below image, Richardson Henry (right) and another worker smooth fresh cement in a biodigester being built at the Lycee Petion in Port-au-Prince. One of four such pilot projects being built in the Belair neighborhood of the earthquake-ravaged city, the tank will use human waste from students at the school, converting it into cooking gas while improving hygiene and health in the neighborhood.

ENA ZIZI IS PULLED ALIVE (above) from the rubble of Haiti's devastating earthquake one week after the city was reduced to ruins in a matter of seconds. The seventy-year old woman was rescued from the collapsed home of the parish priest at Port-au-Prince's Roman Catholic Cathedral of Our Lady of the Assumption by members of a Mexican search and rescue team, several of whom were in tears as they pulled the woman free from tons of rubble. She suffered from dehydration, a dislocated hip, and a fractured leg. In the below image, she gets a drink of water from rescuers.

OSCAR OLIVA, A MEMBER of a Mexican search and rescue team, cries with joy (above) as he embraces a fellow rescuer after the group pulled a seventy-year old woman from the rubble of Haiti's earthquake exactly one week after the tragedy. Oliva is a firefighter from the Mexican city of Quintana Roo. The rescue team is known as "Los Topos"—the moles—and is known internationally for the manner in which it tunnels into rubble to rescue people trapped underneath. In the below image, a victim who wasn't rescued in time is placed on the street for pickup by health officials who carted such bodies off to mass graves.

SILVANI JOSEPH, forty-eight, shows the determined dignity of quake survivors as she carries debris while she and her neighbors begin to build temporary shelters in the Port-au-Prince neighborhood of Belair.

QUAKE AFTERMATH: under the watch of United Nations troops from Argentina, earthquake survivors (above) in the quake-ravaged Haitian city of Leogane unload emergency supplies. In downtown Port-au-Prince, the smell of decomposing bodies makes people (below) cover their faces.

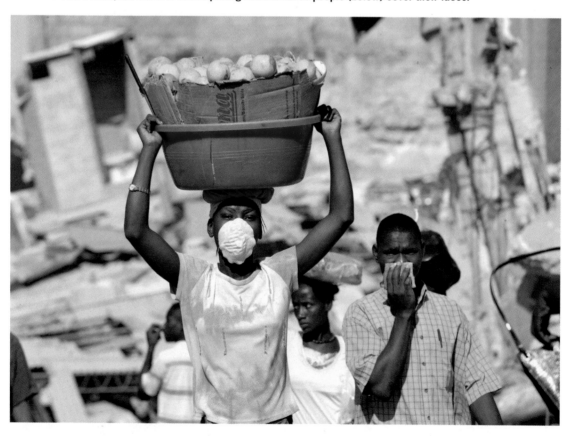

THE MILITARIES FROM MANY COUNTRIES also rushed to lend a hand in the earthquake aftermath. In the above image, U.S. military personnel load a U.S. Navy Blackhawk helicopter in Port-au-Prince with emergency aid for the isolated town of Jacmel on Haiti's southern coast. The aid was provided by Catholic and Protestant churches in Germany, flown to Haiti by the German military, transported across the island by the U.S. Navy, offloaded in Jacmel by Canadian troops, and distributed by a local community-based organization there. In the below image, a small boy from Jacmel is transported back to Port-au-Prince by this U.S. Navy pilot.

A WOMAN (ABOVE) WHO SURVIVED Haiti's earthquake carries water through a camp for homeless families in the Belair section of Port-au-Prince. In the below image, a girl still lives in the Michicu camp for elderly and people living with disabilities, located in Cité Soleil, a poor section of Port-au-Prince, more than one year after the quake.

A WOMAN CARRIES a bundle past a collapsed building in Port-au-Prince, which was devastated by the 2010 earthquake.

AFTER A PORT-AU-PRINCE radio station announced in the wake of the quake that the Canadian Embassy was giving away visas, hundreds of survivors flocked to the embassy, where they were confronted by Canadian soldiers (above). U.S. soldiers, who have a long, checkered history in Haiti, proved themselves useful when aid groups decided to avoid fighting by giving food aid only to women—who then needed to carry it home, getting help from this U.S. soldier (middle). And in Leogane, United Nations troops from Argentina kept the crowd back (bottom) while church groups prepared an aid distribution.

CHILDREN WERE AMONG those most vulnerable to the quake's ravages. Rose Michel, a ten-year-old survivor (above), lost both her legs when the Leogane orphanage she was living in collapsed. Here she plays with other children in the orphanage, which since shortly after the quake has been run by a team of volunteers from the Dominican-Haitian Women's Movement (MUDHA). In the below image, a mother bathes her daughter in a tent city in the Belair neighborhood of Port-au-Prince.

SOON AFTER THE QUAKE, children practice capoeira in a camp for homeless families in the Belair section of Port-au-Prince. The program, run by Viva Rio, a Brazilian nongovernmental organization, was designed to help children affected by the quake recover their emotional well-being.

FOREIGN VOLUNTEERS came to help in many ways after the 2010 quake. Eline Medjune, five, a girl in a Leogane orphanage who survived the earthquake, got special attention from Elena Bargo, a Spanish woman who lives in New York and helped care for the children as a volunteer with the Dominican-Haitian Women's Movement (MUDHA).

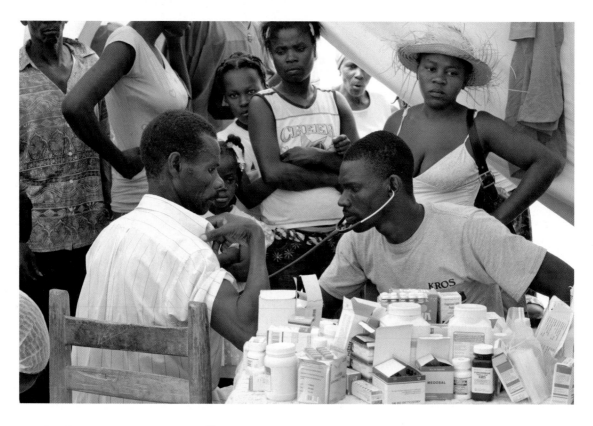

EMERGENCY RESPONSE: Dr. Gaspar Gaston attends patients (above) in a tent clinic set up after the quake on a street in the southern city of Jacmel. In the below image, emergency workers for Norwegian Church Aid, a member of the ACT Alliance, unroll piping in Port-au-Prince as they set up a potable water system for families left homeless by the quake.

VOLUNTEERS MOVE BUCKETS of food and other emergency supplies (above) into the Santa Teresa camp for quake survivors in Petionville. In the middle image, a distribution of food, tents, and other emergency supplies dissolved into chaos when a group of men from a neighboring village invaded a distribution organized by the Lutheran World Federation in the village of Gressier. A police woman fired two shots into the air, motivating the crowd to flee. In the below image, police officers carefully control the crowd in order to avoid a similar scene in the Santa Teresa camp in Petionville.

A MAN FASTENS TOGETHER a temporary shelter for his family in a spontaneous camp for quake survivors being constructed in Croix-des-Bouquets, north of the capital Port-au-Prince.

FAMILIES WHO SURVIVED the quake constructed temporary shelters in the Belair section of Port-au-Prince.

WOMEN CONSTRUCT TEMPORARY homes for their families in a spontaneous camp for quake survivors established in Croix-des-Bouquets immediately following the 2010 earthquake.

HUNDREDS OF EARTHQUAKE SURVIVORS huddle together in tents and makeshift shelters in a soccer stadium in the Santa Teresa area of Petionville, but being victims of the quake didn't mean they had lost their sense of identity. In many places (above), they named the narrow passages between their shelters with street names. In the below image, a girl sweeps one of the dirt paths that wind through the Petionville Camp, where some fifty thousand residents are packed onto what was once a golf course. It's the largest camp of hundreds of locales hosting families left homeless by the 2010 quake.

| **A CAMP FOR HOMELESS** quake survivors set up on a golf course in Port-au-Prince.

A MAN CARRIES scavenged roofing material, and a woman carries a basket of produce to market through the devastated center of Port-au-Prince.

A GIRL BRUSHES HER TEETH in a camp for homeless families set up on a golf course in Port-au-Prince, and boys play as they push a wheelbarrow through a camp in Grand-Goave.

MARIOLETTE SOUFFRANT HELPS her son Lucien Scheinder get dressed for school (above, left) in a tent city in the Mais Gate neighborhood of Port-au-Prince. The four-year-old boy is a student at the Notre Dame de Petits School, run by the Russian Orthodox Church. And rubble gets cleaned up in Port-au-Prince as part of a cash-for-work program (above, right), while in the rural village of Embouchure, a quake-damaged school sponsored by the Episcopal Church is demolished (below) in order to build a new one.

WOMEN WERE LEFT MORE VULNERABLE than ever after the quake. In the above image, women line up for food from the World Food Program in a distribution from which men were excluded, a strategy which reduced violence dramatically. In the below image, Remilliene Morris, a fifty-two-year-old earthquake survivor, sits sadly in her temporary shelter in the Petionville Camp. After her rented home collapsed in the quake, Morris sent two of her four children to live with relatives in the north of the country. Now she struggles to find the school fees for her other two children. She has received donated food and worked occasionally in a cash-for-work program, but lives in ragged clothing and sews together her family's shoes with scavenged string. Morris gets depressed by the continuing struggle to survive.

A MAN BREAKS APART CONCRETE of what was once the Italian Embassy in Port au Prince (above). Destroyed by the 2010 earthquake, the building is now a source of rebar and other salvaged building materials for enterprising recyclers. In the below image, survivors in Port-au-Prince clean up rubble in a cash-for-work program.

A SURVIVOR OF HAITI'S DEVASTATING earthquake, Kesnel Resilia works on building a new house in Leogane (left), a project supported by the Christian Reformed World Relief Committee, a member of the ACT Alliance. In the below image, Beatrice Jean Louis hangs laundry in front of her new house in the same community.

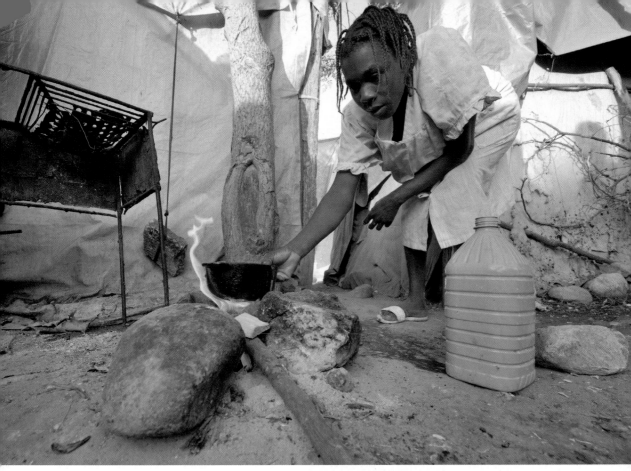

LIFE IN THE CAMPS: a woman heats water for a meager breakfast for her family in a camp in Grand-Goave (above), while in the Corail resettlement camp north of Port-au-Prince, Lorette Beauvoit sets out her wet laundry (below) to dry on the ground around her tent.

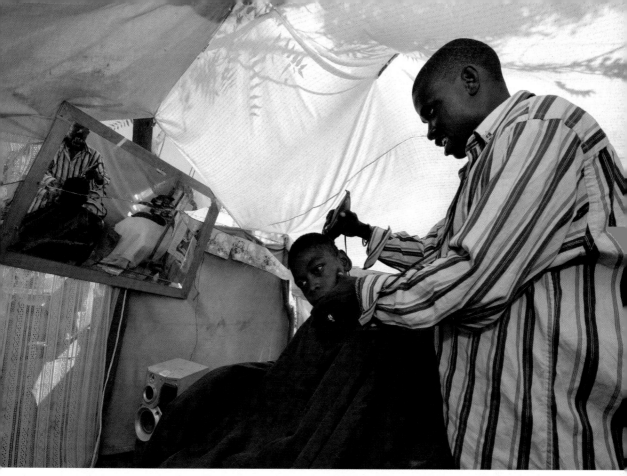

THE LARGEST TEMPORARY CAMP for quake survivors is located on a former nine-hole golf course at the edge of Port-au-Prince (below). The camp has taken on a quasi-permanent state, with businesses, including this barber shop (above), scattered among the tents.

A SURVIVOR OF HAITI'S DEVASTATING EARTHQUAKE, Olginne Pierre sits with her daughter, Olginnes, and her son, Josue, in front of a new house in Leogane, south of the capital of Port-au-Prince. The houses here were built with assistance from the Christian Reformed World Relief Committee, a member of the ACT Alliance.

FRANCISCA MEZUNET, an eight-year-old earthquake survivor (left), participates in activities at a youth center run by the YWCA in Petionville. The program educates and empowers girls (below), many of whom don't go to school, who come from families affected by the 2010 quake. Many live in tents that fill a nearby park.

PEOPLE LIVING WITH DISABILITIES were among those most vulnerable to the quake, including Anouk Nöel (above), who has to use a wheelchair and lost most of her Port-au-Prince house to the quake, and girl students (below) in the Foyer d'Amour d'Haiti, an Orthodox Church–sponsored school for mentally challenged children in the Fontamara neighborhood of Port-au-Prince.

EDNA CORRENORD (above) applies makeup to the face of Marie Michelle Clerirl in a beautician training program at the "House of Hope," a community-based educational training program in Port-au-Prince for children performing domestic work (so-called "restaveks"), sponsored by the Ecumenical Foundation for Peace and Justice. Participants in the program also include former gang members and teenage mothers. Many rights activists consider the use of restaveks to be a modern form of slavery. They are usually children from extremely poor families who are sent away to work as domestic servants in wealthier homes. The children aren't paid for their work, but are provided shelter and meager food. In the best case scenarios, families will send their restavek children to school. But restaveks often work long days performing a variety of household tasks for nothing more that a meal or two a day. Two-thirds of restaveks are girls, and they are extremely vulnerable to rape and sexual abuse from the families who house and control them.

TWO STYLES OF PRESENCE: a Baptist pastor preaches to earthquake survivors (above) huddled in tents and makeshift shelters in a park in the Nerette area of Petionville, while Father Barnabas, a Greek Orthodox priest in the Bobin neighborhood of Port-au-Prince (below), visits with residents of a tent city in his parish.

YOUNG WOMEN RESPOND enthusiastically as U.S. Christian musician Michael W. Smith sings to a crowd in Port-au-Prince. In the below image, a counselor talks to a man who responded to the altar call that concluded a service led by conservative U.S. evangelist Franklin Graham on the one-year anniversary of the quake.

SURVIVORS WORSHIP TOGETHER in Port-au-Prince two weeks after the 2010 quake (above). Local artisans painted colorful Stations of the Cross inside the Sacred Heart Catholic Church in Mizak (below).

HOLDING PHOTOS of family members killed in the disaster (left) and rosary beads (below), Haitians pray during a Catholic Mass in Port-au-Prince marking the one-year anniversary of the 2010 earthquake.

CHILDREN WALK HOME from school in the Haitian village of Foret des Pins (above), while children study in a quake-damaged school building in the village of Embouchure (below).

FATHER JEAN-CHENIER DUMAIS, a Russian Orthodox priest in Port-au-Prince, stands with children of the Notre Dame de Petits school (above) while they sing the national anthem as Haiti's flag is raised at the beginning of a school day. The school's building collapsed in the 2010 earthquake, and classes are currently conducted in the large tents in the background. In the below image, students inside the school.

THE MAIN STREET OF SAINT-MARC (above). In the left image, a woman in Mizak irons recycled cement bag paper to assemble into a notebook, a project of Haitian Artisans for Peace International which generates income for poor families.

RURAL RESIDENTS: a child in Mizak, and a woman washes laundry in Foret des Pins.

PORT-AU-PRINCE RESIDENTS: a woman walks in Cité Soleil, and a marketwomen after a heavy rainstorm in the Croix-des-Bossales market in the La Saline neighborhood.

CHILDREN PLAY SOCCER (above) in what was once the swimming pool of the Italian Embassy in Port au Prince. Destroyed by the 2010 earthquake, the building is now a source of rebar and other salvaged building materials for enterprising recyclers, and the pool a convenient playground for children who live in the Narret Camp for homeless quake survivors, which surrounds the rubble. In the left image, a Brazilian instructor helps a Haitian boy learn capoeira, an Afro-Brazilian dance form, at a community center in the Belair neighborhood of Port-au-Prince.

99

A GIRL CARES FOR HER LITTLE SISTER in the mountain village of Foret des Pins (left), while a family in the village of Dabonne stands in front of the temporary shelter (below) they built following the destruction of their home in the 2010 earthquake. They used old lumber salvaged from the ruins of their previous house.

A BOY FLIES A KITE (left) in a camp for homeless families in Jacmel, a town on Haiti's southern coast that was ravaged by the 2010 earthquake, while boys work in a field in Mare Rouge (below), in the isolated and arid northwest portion of the Caribbean island nation.

A MAN AND HIS DAUGHTER in a camp for quake survivors in Jacmel, on Haiti's southern coast.

Christians. But the inevitable impatience and anger were starting to surface because some aid deliveries had not gone well—with desperate people stampeding for food, for example. Rising anger was inevitable: "What you'll see is that survivors and aid workers are working eighteen-hour days, are dead tired and traumatized," said a security specialist who told me what to expect in the coming days. There was a degree of order now, perhaps because of that very trauma, but in the long term, he predicted, "insecurity is expected to increase; criminals are reorganizing themselves in the camps, and there is already fear of unrest in the camps." Indeed, violent criminals had escaped from prisons in the initial chaos; they had infiltrated the displacement areas, returning to neighborhoods and one-time haunts, and had terrorized remote rural areas, committing rapes, robberies, and murders.

What the security specialist did not say, however, was that part of that anger stemmed from unhappiness and *long-standing* resentment of NGOs themselves. That was hardly surprising—Haiti had long been called the "Republic of NGOs," a place where, even before the quake, three-quarters of human services were provided by nongovernmental groups. While services by some were exemplary, others were scattershot and poorly run. Personnel varied from trained specialists to volunteers who often had little experience. I had seen this in other parts of the world—it wasn't uncommon to see young humanitarian workers who often seemed shockingly ill-prepared for conditions in desperately harsh areas. But the sheer number of humanitarian workers in Haiti was staggering: there have been estimates of as many as 10,000 agencies working in Haiti. That had much to do with the fact that, in the wake of an increasingly weakened state in the decade between 2000 and 2010—with Haiti having no resources for social services—NGOs had become, in effect, "a state within a state."

Such power inevitably invites criticism—as it should—and prompts charges that aid is not getting to Haitian beneficiaries. Some disillusioned aid workers, like Timothy Schwartz in his book *Travesty in Haiti,* have argued that NGOs are, in the end, only dedicated to serving themselves. Too often, Schwartz argues, aid is "being squandered on shoddy, poorly thought-out, and even damaging projects in which no one (is) held accountable." Three months after the quake, President Préval echoed that idea, saying: "All of the millions of dollars that are coming into Haiti right now are going into the hands of NGOs." (Similar criticisms were made about outside construction firms, be they from the United States or the neighboring Dominican Republic.) While NGOs have defended their work over the years, there is still a feeling among Haitians that they have much to answer for—that many development programs have, by and large, failed.

It is likely that few non-Haitian humanitarian workers, at least those going to Haiti for the first time, were initially aware of these tensions and debates. That's not unusual. The idea of humanitarian neutrality—to provide assistance based only on need—is certainly sound, but its downside is a kind of ahistoricity, which can ignore the complexities and layers of Haitian reality and history and replace them with snap judgments and generalities like "the government is inept," or "things here are inefficient." That is why it was satisfying to work with veteran workers like Prospery Raymond of Christian Aid and Sylvia Raulo, then the country representative for the Lutheran World Federation (LWF), who understood the nuances of Haiti and also never lost a sense of their humanity amid chaos.

In the initial days of January 2010, for example, Raulo, who is Finnish, expressed some of the continuing shock and horror of the situation. It was not only the shocking number of a quarter million dead and more than a million displaced that moved her: she and her colleagues had to respond to the disaster, even as they were dealing with their own losses of friends, workers, and family. Three-quarters of Raulo's staff had been displaced and were living on the streets. LWF staffers spent some part of the first days after the quake trying to find their colleagues. "Everyone here is dealing with this loss of life," Raulo said.

But in the midst of such personal challenges came a series of demands and pressures. One constant would be in meeting the demands for accountability from those who contributed financially to the disaster response in Haiti. In a global environment, Raulo acknowledged, donors are rightly concerned about whether aid is getting to those who need it and they require reports and communication. It's a concern that is both legitimate and welcome. Nonetheless, Raulo and her colleagues felt their primary commitment had to be to the Haitians themselves. "We are accountable, first and foremost, to the survivors living in Haiti," she said, "and *then* to those abroad giving and pledging money."

Hard to grasp the working challenges of Haiti

Sylvia Raulo did not downplay the challenges, either in Haiti or with the humanitarian response. She candidly acknowledged that challenges like government corruption and the unpredictability of daily events were not making the distribution of assistance any easier. She also said outsiders probably could not fully grasp the working challenges of a country where the functioning government, in effect, perished in the quake. Thousands of government leaders and civil servants died, and tens of thousands of documents—such as land titles—had been lost as well. "This has been a major blow," because it had set back a country in which, by the end of 2009 and early 2010, a brief sense of calm, order, and stability had finally been felt after years of political turmoil. Others echoed that sentiment, pointing out that humanitarian groups had made good progress in certain neighborhoods, such as building water and latrine systems, only to have them lost in the quake—these neighborhoods had to start from scratch. Raulo was well aware of this loss. "There were a lot of challenges here before," but the country had survived the previous hurricane season, and it seemed as if "there was some stability, some good." So people were understandably asking, "Why now?" In material terms, a decade had been lost; in terms of lives and social capital maybe two decades—a generation—had been lost. I asked her if she thought violence might erupt eventually out of frustration. She believed it possible, but she retained a certain optimism. All who had survived had been given "a gift of life."

Part of the work involves chaos

Still, Raulo's concern about violence, government corruption, and the unpredictability of events proved prescient. The day after I spoke to her, I joined some LWF workers at a distribution in the village of Gressier, located about fifteen miles west of Port-au-Prince. This was the first assistance people in the village and the surrounding area had received— and it was also the first time LWF had worked in the village. Despite the fact that aid was arriving more than two weeks after the quake, those waiting in line were orderly and quiet. I asked Marie Thérèse, who was newly widowed by the quake, how she thought residents in the area were coping. "It's like we're in a desert," she said. But she also praised the work of the young Haitians in charge of the distribution: "They're bringing good support for us." John Charles, an artist and teacher whose school, College Marie Anne, had collapsed in the quake, stood nearby in line for supplies (including a tent) that would provide some needed comfort for himself, his mother, sister, and two cousins. He said people were "patient because they are in need." It was midafternoon; Charles and others had been in line since about eleven that morning.

Soon the relative order and quiet dissolved: a group of young men who were not on LWF's list of recipients tried to disrupt the distribution. Though it is common practice for humanitarian workers to assess needs and then determine those who are the most vulnerable, not everyone accepts or understands these guidelines. A group of local police officers were called in to control the crowd, but refused to do so because they wanted some of the assistance themselves. They were particularly keen on getting some of the tents. When the Haitian LWF aid workers—much to their credit—refused the demand, the police simply watched and did nothing as some in the frustrated crowd rushed toward the distribution site. Some people grabbed whatever they could. A policewoman fired several shots in the air. It was a chaotic moment, and fortunately it did not get worse. It could have: I saw at least one person brandishing a shotgun.

A few other non-Haitians, including some Europeans and North Americans, were with us and watched in dismay. Some in our group were philosophical, saying incidents like this were common when communities had not yet received assistance; it was simply a part of work in chaotic situations and had to be explained as such. "In the beginning, it's difficult," said one Finnish aid worker. Even so, the Haitians in our group were aghast, even angry. When Garry Auguste, acting that day as my guide and translator, saw two men fighting over a tent, he said to me: "I'm ashamed to be Haitian." The LWF staffers were disappointed, even crushed, that their efforts had not gone as planned. "Yes, it's complicated," said distribution coordinator, Sheyla Marie Durandisse, in frustrated understatement. "There is a lot of pressure on the team." Her colleague, Emmanuela Blain, a medical doctor who had been at another LWF distribution a day earlier, admitted she and other aid workers were more than frustrated—some of them were infuriated, even livid. "Yesterday we had a distribution that was perfect. Perfect," Blain said, kissing the tips of her fingers. At the end of the day, in Port-au-Prince, Raulo praised LWF workers for their patience in a trying and dangerous situation. But she added that the problems in Gressier had to be seen in context—in a situation that can seems bereft of hope, "People are traumatized and we know how people can react in these types of situations."

Humanitarian practice is hard and imperfect work

Outsiders may think that distributions of humanitarian aid after a major disaster occur without a hitch—and sometimes they do. The next day, back in Port-au-Prince, we saw a distribution carried out peacefully, with troops from the 82nd Airborne overseeing security. A secure environment was a key element of success there, as was another distribution, at the Santa Teresa camp in Port-au-Prince. In Santa Teresa, a police officer calmly urged the crowd to be patient and said he would personally stop the distribution if problems began. The officer, Harry Brossard, said the tactic seemed to work. It stemmed from his own desire to see food distributed to those who needed it. "We need food for these people," he emphasized. Another key difference with Gressier: unlike those in Santa Teresa, Gressier residents had not received any assistance up until then—many were simply tired and angry.

Certainly the afternoon in Gressier proved that humanitarian practice is hard and imperfect work—a fact often not fully understood or appreciated by donors and even by nonemergency staff members of humanitarian groups. When compounded by the many challenges posed in Haiti—bad infrastructure even before the quake, the massive scale of damage, and the displacement of thousands of people—some acceptance of imperfection and the need to improvise had become part of aid workers' daily realities. "You need to be patient to do this kind of work," Emmanuela Blain told me later when I asked her about the afternoon in Gressier. You also need to be mindful of the dynamics of dignity. "People are hungry, but they also have pride," said Tommy Bouchiba, acting country director for the German humanitarian agency Diakonie Katastrophenhilfe, recalling a story of U.S. military personnel throwing food from the backs of trucks and from helicopters, with Haitians crying out: "Don't throw us food; we're not animals."

Bobby Waddell, a senior advisor for the Lutheran World Federation who had lived and worked before in Haiti for a number of years, winced when I told him that story. He had been with us that day in Gressier and noted that any number of things can go wrong in a humanitarian crisis. These can include bottlenecks in the aid pipeline, coordination problems, and short staffing. There were also the demanding and difficult preexisting realities in Haiti itself. "It's a special place, a special country; it has its own context. It's chaotic in normal times, and has always been a challenging place to work," he said. Those realities exacerbated what became a unique, catastrophic event—"a direct hit on a capital city which then paralyzed an entire country," he said. The trick, Waddell told me, was in maneuvering around all the difficulties while never losing sight of the need to stay dedicated to the survivors.

When I asked him about the coming one-month anniversary and the other anniversaries that would follow—the six-month, the one-year, and so forth—he was forthright and said the challenges were just beginning—things were not going to get any easier. In the end, almost everyone affected by the quake remained vulnerable in some way: Haiti was facing a rainy season, the threat of storms, floods, and hurricanes. "How do we prepare for those?" Waddell asked. Luckily Haiti fared well during what was a relatively quiet 2010 hurricane season. What it was not spared, however, was an unexpected threat: cholera.

A new challenge: a cholera epidemic

Cité Soleil is arguably Haiti's most notorious neighborhood. Located largely on a landfill that sits close to Port-au-Prince's port, this often flood-ridden, densely populated, heavily politicized area is rife with crime. It contains the highest concentration of voters in Haiti—by one estimate, 5 percent of all registered voters in the country—and was a key area of support for Aristide. It was the site of some of the most acute repression during the post-Aristide years of 2004–2006, serving, in Peter Hallward's words, as a place of containment for Haiti's "human damage," a kind of "secure holding-pen for the people who have suffered most from the effects of Haiti's class war." Ironically, though, the neighborhood's waterfront location and its sheer poverty—with its numerous corrugated steel and cinder-block shacks—spared it some of the earthquake's worst effects.

However, the area was not spared the effects of a serious setback to the country's earthquake recovery: the cholera epidemic that began in October 2010. Some called the three months focused on a new medical problem rather than further earthquake recovery "the lost quarter" of 2010. One of those who knew this all too well was Sister Marcella Catozza, a hearty, plainspoken Italian Franciscan who had to stop her other medical work in October, labor through the Christmas season, and was still dealing with the epidemic during and after the one-year earthquake commemoration.

Sister Marcella's clinic—a newly rebuilt, brightly painted building—sits on a slight crest overlooking the waterfront and an area pocketed with older, small steel and cinder-block structures; compared to those stark buildings, the new clinic and some new green and blue houses built near it are a welcome, and welcoming, contrast. I asked Charles Wilner, one of several young Haitian volunteers who work with Sister Marcella at the clinic, and is one of those she kiddingly calls "her boys," about the immediate neighborhood, Wharf Jeremie. He said that drugs, alcohol abuse, and violence are a constant in Wharf Jeremie. In many ways, it's lawless: "There are no police here," he said. Stays here tend to be short; the colleague I was with had us packing within an hour—something about the area didn't feel safe, and a team of humanitarian workers who had delivered supplies to Sister Marcella's clinic days before had been robbed.

As for the presence of cholera, Wilner said residents had accepted it as one more fact of life in an unsettled, volatile environment. For her part, though, Sister Marcella betrayed no hint of exhaustion or frustration with having to cope with yet one more problem in what had already been a terrible year: she made a joke about having spent her Christmas holiday with cholera. Not only had she dealt with the maimed and the dying after the earthquake, Sister Marcella also had to rebuild her damaged clinic and struggle to provide health care in an area where many nongovernmental groups still refuse to work because of its notorious reputation.

In the densely populated area surrounding the clinic, cholera had taken a serious toll. In November, Sister Marcella's clinic—which she had originally established as a pediatric care center—had suddenly turned into a cholera treatment center. Her staff was treating eighty patients a day in a facility with half as many beds. As of January 2011, some two thousand cholera patients had been treated at the clinic. Seventeen died—seventeen of the estimated five thousand who had died by April of 2011, a month when public health officials estimated that eventually five hundred thousand would come down with cholera. Two of those at the clinic died in what Sister Marcella recalled as a particularly horrific moment: Early in the epidemic, she arrived at the clinic and found two people barely alive at the front door. Within ten minutes, they were dead. Although the number of patients declined in the weeks before I saw her in mid-January, Sister Marcella expected cases to spike again.

(She was right; when I returned in April 2011, during the onset of the rainy season, cholera cases were on the increase.) She called cholera "unsparing and unpredictable."

Sister Marcella explained that cholera—which can cause severe vomiting and diarrhea and, left untreated, can kill a person within hours—is linked to other problems that have long bedeviled Haiti, including malnutrition and hunger. "Malnutrition is a basic problem for people here," she explained, and those who suffer from a poor diet are more susceptible to cholera. "We need to figure out a way to break this cycle," she said, arguing that temporary "emergency" solutions won't solve long-standing underlying problems. She knew firsthand about the shortfalls of interim measures. The Brazil-based humanitarian group Viva Rio had established temporary portable latrines on her clinic grounds. While welcome, such assistance was unsustainable: the group's high-tech "bio-digester" latrines weren't as practical as simpler, composting toilets. Nearby, another set of latrines, donated by Doctors Without Borders, had been sitting full for weeks, waiting to be cleaned or removed.

Sister Marcella said speculation as to how cholera reached Haiti was understandable, but almost beside the point. It was commonly thought it was brought to Haiti by UN peacekeeping forces, an unpopular group because they are seen as an occupying force. In any case, cholera was now a fact of life in Haiti, just as it is in Sister Marcella's native Italy. "When cholera is in a country, it doesn't leave," she said. "It's a condition of life. Cholera is now endemic to Haiti. It's part of the country now."

✦   ✦   ✦

"You're up against something really, really hard"

That made life all the more difficult for Sister Marcella and Dr. Jean Gardy Marius, a Haitian physician who oversees a rural clinic in Rousseau, about seventy miles north of Port-au-Prince. I joined Dr. Marius on a day at his clinic. During the two-hour trip from Port-au-Prince, he recounted his experiences in treating cholera during the preceding months. While the number of new cholera cases at the rural clinic had declined in recent weeks, Dr. Marius noted that treating the disease is "problematic because it's tied to so many other things, like poor nutrition." While a relatively healthy person can be asymptomatic, an unhealthy person will have serious problems in recovering from cholera. Dr. Marius recalled one cholera patient at his clinic who vomited five gallons of fluid in twenty minutes. "We have so many factors—lack of education, poverty, malnutrition— that you're up against something really, really hard. Very big problems. It has to do with the conditions of the life of the people. Nothing has changed in the last year. People are still living in poverty," Dr. Marius said. He recalled one family's typical experience. One day the children came into the clinic for treatment of cholera; the next day, their parents did. "It was a big mess," he said. Immediate treatment worked, but Marius asked if the family had enough to eat. "The father said, 'We don't have anything. I don't even have one dollar.' You can't do that indefinitely—just giving out oral rehydration salts. The family needs enough to eat, potable water, toilets that work."

Given Haiti's dependence on outside aid and the stillborn attempts to initiate an inexpensive national health system, it's hardly surprising that Marius spoke of frustrations about the overall state of health services: after hearing people say repeatedly that the Haitian government was absent, particularly in impoverished, rural areas, here was someone who was trying his level best to fill the gap. "The government doesn't exist," Marius said. He looked wearily at the road. "The Haitian government doesn't even know how many people live in this country," he said. "We've never had a government that thought about the Haitian people. The government has just worked for their family or friends. There's never been a national policy. Never." He paused again. "You're working against so many factors in this country. People in rural areas—they have nothing. Nothing. They don't have hope. Many people are living by the goodness of God."

What then of the nongovernmental groups like his? Dr. Marius acknowledged what is often said of NGOs in Haiti: some do good, but there are too many of them; they posess too much power; and a number do not do good work. Some "show up in this country, receive money, and then leave," he said. He said he understands the frustration of Haitians who say that little, if anything, had emerged from response of the last year. For many, he said, "It's like it was a week after the quake. For them, what's been done? Nothing." Still, despite all of their attendant problems, he said, the NGOs were still Haiti's only social safety net. "If it weren't for the NGOs, I don't know what the Haitian people would do."

Hoping to build something that will overcome the breach

Small clinics such as Sister Marcella's and Dr. Marius's are limited in what they can do in the absence of a functioning health system—but for those they serve, the clinics are the only health-care safeguards they have. About fifty-two thousand persons are dependent on Dr. Marius's clinic, and Marius acknowledged, "I can't resolve everything. I can only do so much." The clinic's overworked staff must deal not only with cholera, but also with other diseases like malaria. Some people, especially those over forty, have not seen a doctor for years, maybe never. Dr. Marius himself grew up in a poor family, and said that for most of his mother's life, she did not see a doctor. "That was one of my motivations for doing this," he said. Marius doesn't like grandiosity—his strongly held opinions are spoken evenly, softly—but he sees his work at least partially as a way to help those like his mother and also as a way to rebuild a shattered society. He knows that effort will take years, and must overcome a culture of corruption and neglect he says won't be, can't be, solved right away. It could take twenty years, but it has to be done: he compared the health problems in Haiti to a cancer—a cancer that is "killing those in the countryside."

At a rural clinic, long lines

Patients had queued up in a long line alongside a dirt road when we arrived at the clinic at about eight in the morning. A banner overhead read *Pwoteje Lavi Nou* ("Protect Our Lives") and urged local residents to wash their hands after eliminating body waste. Many of those in line were not there for cholera treatment, but had certainly heard about the epidemic and were heeding the warnings about hand-washing and clean water.

Plaisir Carline came to the clinic for treatment of stomach problems. It was her first visit to the clinic, and yes, she was worried about cholera: in her circle of friends, family, and neighbors, twenty people had it. Three people had died. Elphina Frederic said she was suffering from stomach problems, headaches, and a vaginal infection. Exane Genescar, wearing a Detroit Tigers cap, was there because she had a fever and a severe stomachache. Nonetheless, cholera was the talk of her friends and family. "The way people are dying," she said, "yes, that makes me scared."

In a separate tent for cholera patients lay Germilia Omisca, a mother of nine. Her oldest child was twenty-three; she did not know her own exact age. She lives in the nearby village of Coline. Lying in a bed while an intravenous drip replenished her lost fluids, Omisca said she felt much better since her arrival a day earlier. She had had a case of diarrhea, and knew she had lost weight. Omisca had not been eating regularly before becoming ill. There had been times when she didn't eat for several days because she didn't have the money to buy food. Omisca did not know when she would return home and resume her routine as a small merchant and subsistence farmer. I also spoke to Normile Noel, thirty-eight, a farmer and health worker who had been recruited to clean the beds with bleach. He said the clinic was doing much good—sometimes people were carried in on the shoulders of family members, and within a day or two, their condition had greatly improved. Some were flat out in the morning; by afternoon they were at least smiling. Noel confirmed that hunger was clearly a factor in the sickness. As for cholera, "I don't fear it myself," he told me, "because I apply the law of hygiene. I wash my hands."

The other health workers I spoke to, all Haitian, said they were proud of their role in containing the disease in their area. They trekked to nearby small hamlets and villages and told residents to treat water and wash their hands. "Keep it clean," said LaRoche Mildrede. Davidson Noel agreed: "They are afraid, but when we talk to them and tell them it can be prevented and treated, they are relieved. It gives them courage."

I caught up with Dr. Marius in the afternoon and told him I was impressed: He smiled and said, "Our team loves our patients." He recalled that the clinic had treated patients who had had pulses and blood pressure of zero. "You have fifteen minutes to give them the (saline) solution," he said. "Otherwise they die."

The clinic treats about one hundred patients a day, every day of the week, and Dr. Marius said he would like to treat more, particularly given the connection between malnutrition and illnesses, including cholera. A feeding program for children is one of his dreams, as malnutrition is most severe among children: "There is no way for children in Haiti to be healthy," he said. But Dr. Marius does not have the resources to initiate a feeding program. Such a program requires very focused work on relatively large numbers of children. Certainly there would be plenty of children who might benefit: this is a notable hard-scrabble part of Haiti, at least in terms of food—it's hilly and rocky, poor for producing crops. Not having enough to eat is a chronic problem: most Haitians live on less than U.S. $2 a day, and food—much of it imported—is not cheap. "This issue of food security is very challenging," Dr. Marius said. "Most of the people at the clinic are sick because they've been suffering from nutrition problems for years."

For mother and child, the first thousand days are crucial

Problems can begin in pregnancy—many Haitian women will never see a general practitioner, much less an obstetrician during their pregnancies. "A pregnant woman is supposed to consume a certain number of calories each day. But it never happens. She doesn't have the opportunity to get it," Marius said, noting that many do not have the means to buy food. A cycle then begins, with premature births and children without enough food growing up malnourished. Marius's worry is a reflection of a growing consensus among doctors, scientists, and humanitarians that the first thousand days that begin at pregnancy and end roughly at a child's second birthday represent what the British medical journal *Lancet* has called the "golden interval"—the time when health and nutrition interventions for an infant can make the biggest difference for long-term physical and medical health.

"People end up eating whatever they can find." Marius looked at me evenly. "I can say 99 percent of those in rural areas will not get basic services, and that's a risk for so many problems. In this country, a basic functioning health system doesn't exist. People are not even vaccinated properly—it's why they are so vulnerable to malaria and other diseases."

Compounding the problem: a tradition of physicians only speaking in French, putting a distance between them and Kreyòl-speaking Haitians. "People feel the doctors don't respect you if you don't speak French," he said, recalling his mother's experiences with doctors. The issue of respect and dignity is one he takes seriously: "We're to treat people with respect; all of us came from poor families, and there is no reason for us to forget where we came from," he said. "So we treat our patients like they are fathers, our mothers, because there is no difference between them and my mother and father." The issue of dignity is the reason that this clinic is not free; it charges a base fee of 100 gourdes—about U.S. $2.20. "It's good to have to contribute to something," he said. "It's good to have to pay for some services. People do not complain about this or the services we provide." His clinic has outposts in twenty-seven locations, some of which require a seven- to eight-hour walk to get there. The conditions of roads "are a reason why so many people have difficulty getting to us." While most of those I spoke to walked less than an hour to get to the clinic, others began their journeys at three in the morning. And in rural areas like this, walking long distances becomes just one more added burden for the poor.

CHAPTER
7

The Quest for Food Security

Burdens for Haitians became worse after the attendant terrors of the earthquake, which is why the fertile valleys of Haiti's north had beckoned to survivors of the disaster that laid waste Port-au-Prince and other Haitian cities. The peace of this green, quiet country could be a balm for those seeking relief from the capital's congestion and chaos. But the region has many problems that are emblematic of the long-term challenges Haiti faces not only from the earthquake, but also from what Scott Campbell of Catholic Relief Services (CRS) called a "structural disaster that has been there for years"—the issue of food, hunger, and nutrition.

Food security—the access and availability to food, as well as its utilization—was a critical issue before the earthquake and continues to be: Haiti has the worst indicators in the Western Hemisphere for the health of mothers and children under age five. About a quarter of all Haitian children are stunted, a telling sign of malnutrition. A quarter of the population is chronically undernourished; one in five persons dies before age forty.

These sobering and pernicious realities were evident in the early days following the quake; during my initial assignment in Haiti in January 2010, the issue of food was the biggest anxiety I saw and heard. People on the streets motioned with their hands around their stomachs. They were hungry. At a feeding center being run in Port-au-Prince, Judith Jules tended to one of her children, a malnourished six-month-old child. All of the children at the center were thin, some of them stunted or seriously underweight and were receiving supplementary feeding. Mothers talked of joblessness since the quake, of children being sick, of uncertainty about the future. "Things here have been hard. Even more than hard," Jules said.

Rose-Anne Auguste, a Haitian humanitarian and women's activist, was juggling several roles as she dealt with the feeding program, health-care work, and the emerging problem of sexual violence in the camps. But the day I spoke to her, three weeks after the quake, worries over food and hunger commanded most of her attention. In the short-term, that meant supporting women who work as food vendors and helping them to expand their businesses. But Auguste also felt that in the long-term, Haiti needed to develop more reliable food resources on its own. She was adamant about the need for Haiti to become "food independent."

"We've had thirty years of projects and there's been no response to our reality," she said. "Haiti has many structural problems; the international community must understand our reality and match projects with our reality." When I noted the importance of food supplements—like Plumpy'nut, a supplement used in the clinic—as essential in the crucial first thousand-day cycle of nutrition, Auguste agreed that that could be one approach. (Ironically for Haiti, a country where people grow peanuts, the peanut-based supplement is manufactured by a French firm.) But that was only part of a larger solution, she argued. "Haiti has the clear ability to feed itself. We produce good food in this country." She paused. "We are not the state," Auguste said of her group's feeding program. "We cannot resolve the problems of our people. It's why we can only serve five hundred families."

In a naturally fertile valley, a cry for food

Such realities and frustrations are omnipresent in Haiti. Recall the work of Fontil Louiner, the video technician who helped develop the feeding program in Petite Rivière in the northern department, or province, of Artibonite. While the program was an initial success, it had to be downsized as the flight back to Port-au-Prince began, with the result that the feeding program, understandably, had to be reduced to just a few days a week. The realities were these: many people still had family in Port-au-Prince; some still had homes, and humanitarian assistance remained easier to access in the capital. Despite initial talk of decentralizing a heavily centralized nation, there was also a nagging sense that Haiti's future—certainly the immediate future—still belongs in the capital. There was another practical issue: most of those fleeing Port-au-Prince who moved in with "host families" of relatives and friends no longer had any direct ties to the land itself. They were no longer farmers. "Many had no sustainable economic activities in these rural areas—they had nothing to do—and so they left their host households," said CRS food security advisor Dina Brick. "They may have also wanted to reduce the strain they recognized they were bringing to their host families."

The pressures and strains are real; a postquake survey of households outside of Port-au-Prince by Catholic Relief Services and other humanitarian groups indicated that families were cutting back on their daily meals—nearly half of households reported the number of meals dropped from two and a half a day to one and a half. That reduction, Brick added, was "a sign of serious stress, and of continued vulnerability for a large number of households." The Petite Rivière feeding program experienced similar problems. Keeping the program going came up against a long-standing reality: Petite Rivière itself has had long-standing difficulties in feeding itself. The irony, even tragedy, of the situation is that, as Rose-Anne Auguste said about Haiti as a whole, Petite Rivière sits amid plenty. The Artibonite Valley is sometimes called Haiti's "rice bowl," but many of its residents are no strangers to hunger. Sama Odmarc, a teacher and journalist I met during an afternoon at the studios of the radio station that helped coordinate the feeding program, said, "We're in great need of food here."

Why is Haiti hungry?

How did this happen? For years, there has been debate over whether it was wise for Haiti to embark on a policy of neoliberal trade liberalization in which the United States and U.S.-dominated multilateral organizations like the World Bank and the International Monetary Fund demanded that the Haitian government implement a program in which Haiti, first, would be transformed into an export-based economy, with greater economic interdependence with the United States, and, second, peasants would, as Timothy Schwartz notes in *Travesty in Haiti*, "be transformed into factory workers." Concurrent with that, Schwartz notes, and in the wake of the political chaos of the mid-1980s, Haiti—a country proudly self-sufficient in producing rice and where an astonishing one in five was once directly involved in the production of the crop—fully reversed course. Tariffs in place to protect Haitian rice farmers fell, and U.S. rice flooded the market.

By 1996, Schwartz notes, "2,100 metric tons of U.S. rice arrived in Haiti every week, an annual loss to impoverished Haitian cultivators of about 23 million dollars per year." The consequences of that policy were dire to Haiti's poor, resulting in what Schwartz called "the near total destruction of the agricultural economy. Ships left Haitian ports empty and returned with their holds packed with thousands of tons of United States, German, and French surplus and subsidized wheat, rice, corns, and beans. Meanwhile, throughout Haiti one could find avocadoes, oranges, and even mangos rotting on the ground or being fed to pigs."

Proponents of the liberalization measures have argued that reform was needed to stabilize the country after years of political and social upheaval. The Haitian government "had no choice but to open its economy as part of the policy reforms proposed," acknowledged a 2006 study by Christian Aid that criticized the results of trade liberalization. The study noted that the practical outcomes of such reforms—reducing tariffs on imported food, for example—had some positive results for urban residents who benefited from cheaper food prices. But the overall social cost to Haiti has been grave, the Christian Aid study concluded. Once self-sufficient in food, Haiti was, by 2006, importing food more than any other product, and was using 80 percent of its export earnings to pay for food imports. There has long been speculation that these policies were pushed on then-President Aristide as a condition for U.S. support for his return to power. For his part, former President Bill Clinton—in his capacity as United Nations special envoy on Haiti—has since apologized for policies while he was president that benefited rice farmers in his native Arkansas, but were not good for a country that once *exported* rice.

The concomitant loss of agricultural production has crippled rural areas like Artibonite, where the loss of farm income makes it hard for people to feed themselves. "In this environment, it is becoming more and more difficult to buy food," the 2006 study said. "Agricultural liberalization has contributed to hunger becoming more widespread in both rural and urban areas." These related pressures are all too familiar in Petite Rivière and Artibonite, where imported rice has continued to erode the domestic rice industry, putting increased pressure on local farmers, who still find it hard to compete in a market flooded by cheap rice.

Farmers are increasingly burdened as they try to secure credit for basics like fertilizer, making it more difficult for them to diversify their crops, narrowing what people can eat. The local diet, residents say, is heavy on rice, corn meal, sweet potatoes, and millet, but contains too little protein. While the long-term issues of food and hunger in rural areas were, understandably, never highlighted during the media coverage of the various anniversaries of the earthquake, they deserve to be, said Scott Campbell, who helped oversee Catholic Relief Services' reconstruction and recovery efforts in Haiti. "Nothing in this emergency can be looked at in isolation," said Campbell, noting that in the long run, food security is part of a "web of complexity" that, in effect, lies just below the current catastrophe—a "structural disaster" that not only encompasses food and hunger, but the related issues of poverty, corruption, and weak governance.

A long-term solution: Haiti should produce its own food

Eliminating hunger and food insecurity could prove to be a cornerstone to solving many of Haiti's seemingly intractable problems. "A long-term solution is for Haiti to produce its own food," Campbell of CRS said. The World Food Program, the food distribution arm of the United Nations, was among the agencies moving beyond emergency food assistance to develop what it calls a "longer-term food security strategy" that includes generating more localized production by Haitian farmers. Other strategies being discussed include addressing the issue of affordable credit as well as supporting food cooperatives as a way to boost local food supplies. The key, many argue, lies in opening up economic opportunities outside of Port-au-Prince. When people in rural areas have to flee to Port-au-Prince just to make a living, "making investments in agricultural requirements such as good seed, tools, and fertilizer could turn this tide and redistribute Haiti's population in a more sustainable way and also empower Haitians to meet their own food security needs," said Lisa Rothenberger, who heads the humanitarian relief program for the American Baptist Churches, a U.S. Protestant denomination.

The need to retool rural areas and decentralize the country were much-talked about when Fontil Louiner and his colleagues huddled in Radio Family's small studio after the earthquake and spoke of the problems facing Petite Rivière. They discussed what Louiner called "the issue of rice"—how a once-flourishing industry had been destroyed. In my return visit to Petite Rivière in mid-2010, these concerns were even more pronounced. The issue of food touched everything. Those around the table at the radio studio—farm advocates and activists—mentioned the real and palpable challenges of the lack of reasonable farm credit and of recovering from a cycle of hurricanes in recent years that caused massive flooding and crippled the region. This accumulation of one obstacle after another was confirmed by Arnold Alcimé, an octogenarian farmer. After greeting visitors to his small two-acre plot of land, Alcimé rattled off a long list of worries facing him and other farmers: drainage problems in the face of increased floods; "usury" loans that constantly keep him and others mired in debt; the exorbitant cost of new equipment.

Activists like agronomist Nicolas Altidor and the Rev. Raymond Mesadieu believe better and expanded options for farmers are necessary. "It's something simple," said Altidor. "Help the planters, give them what they need—fertilizer, access to reasonable credit, and improved drainage so that fields are not always flooding." Mesadieu believes that the government should do these things. But none of them had faith that the Haitian government would, or could, do anything to assist small farmers. "No, no, no," the men said in unison. Such pessimism is not unusual, of course, though it is balanced by the day-to-day grit and determination of Haitians as they go about their lives amid great difficulties.

The CRS survey gave a picture of some of those daily challenges. One finding was that Haitian women—important traders and vendors in their local economies, who sell fruit, candies, gum, and the like—were finding it hard to maintain their small-scale vending "due either to a lack of demand, or increasing difficulties gaining credit, or higher repayment rates," said food security expert Brick of CRS. Brick, among others, echoed the opinion of the farm activists in Petite Rivière that, at the least, efforts must be made to support small farm families. "At the same time, we need to invest more in building alternative economic options for poor farmers," she said, with an eye on reducing Haiti's dependence on imports.

Whatever is done, life must be made easier and better for rural Haitians, said the residents of Petite Rivière, who expressed frustration about the country's almost maddening centralization. Even getting a driver's license requires a costly trip to Port-au-Prince. If people could stay in rural areas, they would. "But there's still a feeling," said agronomist Altidor, "that you can make more money in the city than here in the provinces."

The centralization of Haitian society into Port-au-Prince is an enormous stumbling block, and the long-term issue of "building up" rural Haiti will take years to sort out. Indeed, it may take a lot of time, if the experience of twenty-year-old Datus Raynashca is any indication. When I met her in July of 2010, Raynashca joined with others in Petite Rivière who gathered for an afternoon meal of white rice and black beans, part of the scaled-down feeding program. Raynashca told of being displaced from Port-au-Prince along with her father. She doubted she would, or even could, remain in Petite Rivière. An aspiring secretary, she still feels the pull of the capital. Of life in Petite Rivière, she said, "There is nothing here"—an example of a young person from a rural area with a contribution to make to her home area but unable to stay there.

But six-year-old David Jean Datus, who lost a leg in the quake and moved with his family to Petite Rivière, said he would like to be a farmer and doesn't believe being physically handicapped can stop him. "I want to grow plantains," he said of the banana common in Haiti and the Caribbean. As a lunch ended, with dishes to be washed and the cooks scraping off the heavy pans, the Rev. Raymond Mesadieu, the community activist who works on behalf of local farmers, reminded a group of visitors what constitutes security in rural Haiti. "There's education," he said, noting its extreme importance. But then "there's nutrition," Mesadieu said—the stuff of life itself.

At a mountainous food cooperative, signs of hope

The rice fields of Artibonite can resemble Asia's fertile valleys; its mountains can resemble Colorado's foothills. And like the hills and low mountains of the American West, Haiti's are marked by a welcome quiet, calm, and stillness, particularly after Port-au-Prince's chaos, congestion, and noise. The sky is bluer here, the air crisper. At the end of an afternoon or the start of the morning, the soft mountain light almost glows. It's a region that evokes the well-known Kreyòl phrase *Dèyè mòn, gen mòn*—"Beyond the mountain are more mountains." Climbing the mountains is not easy—the trail is rough—and stories of shouldering people up and down mountains to get them to a doctor are legion; it's not uncommon to hear that people have died along the way. The nearest nurse is about two to three hours away.

When you get to the top of one of these mountains, at Mayombe, you are met by residents wearing parkas and relatively heavy clothing; this is cold for Haiti. But the chill in the air soon disappears. People are happy to see and host you and talk about a social experiment—food cooperatives that began in the 1990s with ties to the Lavalas movement that sought to bring some social and economic stability for rural residents. The co-ops' governing philosophy is simple: "It's the state's responsibility to develop the country, but as the state has failed to do that, we've decided to take the initiative." Lessage Jacques Issalien is one of the founders of the "Hand in Hand" cooperative, in which members have small plots, pool their resources for buying seeds and land, and grow crops both for themselves and for sale at market. Small profits have also allowed the co-op to provide small loans for developing nurseries and the raising of livestock. Some co-op members own land, and some do not, renting from fellow co-op members. U.S. churches and U.S.-based development agencies, including Church World Service and the Foods Resource Bank, are providing support, though the eventual goal is for the cooperatives to become fully self-sufficient.

Co-op members are proud of their ability to be self-sustaining

For two days, co-op members hosted me and some other visiting colleagues. What was immediately apparent was how everyone seemed more relaxed than residents of Port-au-Prince, giving rise to a joke: when you ask what time it is, people reply, "The same time it was yesterday." Yet there was still an element of bustle: residents were restoring nurseries and gardens that had been damaged by Hurricane Tomas several months earlier. The area is prone to the ill effects of hurricanes because of heavy deforestation; reforestation efforts are now a priority for the community (and for much of Haiti), because for years trees have been used for making charcoal, the main source for cooking in Haiti. Climate change has added to the sense of urgency about the problem: changing climate and deforestation have made flooding during hurricane seasons worse than in years past. While Haiti was spared large-scale damage during the 2010 hurricane season, previous years had brought severe flooding to the area—one of the reasons why developing nurseries and planting trees, as well as building forests again, is so important.

About three dozen co-op members met us at a school to explain their work and praised the progress and assess continuing challenges. One such issue: the community's isolation and inaccessibility, which makes access to health care very difficult. "It's a major problem. We're not doctors, we don't have experience with this," Issalien said. Sometimes a health worker from a clinic comes in and provides first-aid training. "But that's not enough." The community's wish is to have a health center, he added, "but we haven't found a solution to that yet."

While health care remains a major hurdle, members were proud of the progress that had been made: pooling resources and developing access to much-needed credit, loans, and seeds. Co-op members were clearly proud of their ability to be self-sustaining, of storing crops and seeds for use, with enough left over to send to market and earn some income. Among the vegetables and fruits they grow are chives, garlic, potatoes, bananas, yams, sweet potatoes, sugar cane, yucca, avocadoes, and mangos.

While outside groups provided emergency assistance during crises like Hurricane Tomas, the co-op members felt they were, as Issalien described it, a small self-governing "state within a state." "We have a lot of authorities here," he said, suggesting in effect, that everyone is, in effect, a boss with an equal say—the community acts democratically.

It certainly acts in an open and welcoming way—the co-op had served as a refuge for Port-au-Prince earthquake survivors in the last year. More than one hundred former residents who had, through the years, moved to Port-au-Prince returned after the earthquake. As was the case in Artibonite, most eventually returned to the capital—the pull of Port-au-Prince is still strong—but about twenty-five remained permanently. For those who had concluded that life in Port-au-Prince was no longer for them, finding in the co-op a place of respite, sanctuary, and shelter had been crucial. While she acknowledged that she missed some aspects of life in Port-au-Prince, Ophliase Joseph said she realized that life in the capital was no longer tenable for her and her family. "We're all staying here," Joseph said of her new life in Mayombe.

Another woman who returned to Mayombe was Nocile St. Juliun Fortuna. She had left the region in 1995 to work in Port-au-Prince, where her husband had found work as a mason. Like many other transplanted women, Fortuna sold small food items on the streets. On January 12, 2010, she was outside, looking for water, when the earthquake struck. Though their home was destroyed, the family survived. "In less than ten days we decided to come back here," she said, adding that with a collapsed home and no job opportunities, it was time to leave the capital and return to Mayombe.

"I had no hope," she said. "None." Once she arrived back, she had to find something to support her family. With a loan, she was able to purchase items like cooking oil and beans that she could resell at a small profit and support the family. She makes her payments monthly and will have the loan paid off by October of 2011. "I've become more hopeful, yes," she said, noting that she is one of fifty women who have received loans as part of a self-governing group. That has been empowering. Still, she considers being back home and part of the cooperative a blessing. "I couldn't have done this on my own," she said. Senicia Sidoine, forty-seven, another one-time resident who fled Port-au-Prince after the quake and the death of her husband, praised the co-op's support: schooling for her family and help when she needed medical care and medicine. "The co-op," she said, "is the only family we have."

People have done what the government should do but does not

Cher-Frere Fortune, a coordinator of the cooperatives who works with the Christian Center for Integrated Development in Port-au-Prince, has worked with the co-op since its founding in 1992. He is one of a number of Haitians who struck me as having the leadership potential to enter politics—a fact confirmed by founder Issalien, who declared: "If we had ten leaders like Cher-Frere in Haiti, we'd have major improvements in the country." The quiet, self-effacing but confident Fortune says he and others like him are more effective on the outside. "I don't want to be president," Fortune told me. "If I were president, I could not help people the way I do."

The work of Fortune, forty-two, stems from a belief—born from frustration, he acknowledges—that the issue of food and hunger in Haiti has a distinct "political undertone to it, because the government is not present and does not have a system to provide agricultural credit to peasants." An operative, functioning state—a structured state—should have the ability "to bring services to the areas where people live." The Haitian government can't do this. "That's one of the weaknesses of the current government." So people in rural areas have organized and, with the assistance of NGOS, have done what the government should do but does not—provide credit so that farmers can buy seeds and farm animals, make changes and improvements, and have a solid foundation on which to live. "I have a definition of food security," Fortune told me. "To me, it's as simple as having enough to eat on a daily basis. It shouldn't be foods that are imported, but foods people raise themselves and in enough quantity so they have enough for a rainy day and enough so they have enough resources until the next planting season." There should be no exceptions to this rule.

Certainly, that has been easier said than done. In a remote area like this, there was a dynamic in which people "were looking for a savior; they were waiting for the government. But when the government didn't come, they realized that wasn't the solution: they had to look to themselves and come together and join forces." I asked Fortune if he thought people in the co-op viewed him as their leader. He answered, "No. They know it's theirs. They manage it; it's not other people running it; they are the owners and the managers." Does he think the cooperative model could work elsewhere in Haiti? Perhaps, though he added the times after the earthquake and after Hurricane Tomas were not ideal to begin co-ops. True, outside assistance was needed after both events. But the amounts needed after the quake and after Tomas were not large. All in all, he believes that the food cooperatives have dramatically reduced the amount of outside aid needed by a community.

It's a chain of solidarity

Elvius St. Fulis agrees. He left Mayombe for Port-au-Prince in 1995, a year he remembers for its difficulties. "Things were terrible for farming here then, and we couldn't make a living." So he made the journey to Port-au-Prince, a city he never much liked. He never settled into life in the capital, where he worked as a bread seller; he returned to Mayombe in 2001 and joined the cooperative, taking up farming.

Like Fortuna, St. Fulis wishes the cooperative had more resources—he and others can often "only break even." To survive means juggling some things: having to rent out land, selling produce in the market. When I met St. Fulis, he and others were harvesting mélanga—a root vegetable. A school is a ninety-minute walk away, but St. Fulis is proud his children are attending. "That will open the door for them, to have success."

I asked him what concrete changes had taken place as a result of the co-op. St. Fulis said that before the cooperatives, people were hungry and dependent on the uncertainty of seasonal harvests. "That's why we thought there was a need; when we planted sweet potatoes, we'd have to wait five months; spices three months." With cooperative sharing and storage, it became possible to rely less and less on the immediate harvest. Also, pressures eased because the cooperative was able to provide more seeds, which allowed more planting and harvesting. "There is less hunger than before, that's for sure," he said. St. Fulis paused. "It's a chain of solidarity. Everyone is involved in the process—women, men. As a body, we're not dependent on the government. It's good to be self-reliant." The co-op has meant long-term development, he said. "It means life to us."

8

Haiti's God Talk

During Holy Week 2011, with the immediate urgency of the quake and its aftermath long past, I had a bit more free time than I had had during previous assignments. So I asked friends and colleagues about trying to see a Voodoo ceremony. I wanted to explore the religion that had been so often alluded to by so many. No one seemed surprised by my request—Voodoo (or Vodou as it is also spelled) is an endless source of fascination for outsiders. Haitians I met were either fairly casual and matter-of-fact about it, or downplayed Voodoo's significance—in both cases, perhaps, to minimize its exotic, dangerous reputation in the imagination of non-Haitians.

I was told Holy Week might not be the best time to see a ceremony—one lay Roman Catholic told me it was common for Voodoo priests and priestesses to lay low during Holy Week. But I actually saw a number of music-laced "Ra ra" Voodoo processions during that time—processions that my Church World Service colleague Burton Joseph, an Episcopalian, said symbolize the syncretism between the Voodoo and Christian traditions. Christians, of course, commemorate the Lenten season by attending church, praying, and fasting, while non-Christian Haitians "in their own way celebrate the same season," he said. "Every saint from the church is represented by a corresponding spirit in the Voodoo religion—though under a different name, of course."

The various and colorful evocations of God's gifts are not surprising in a country where Christianity and indigenous religions mix, seamlessly to some, and sometimes uneasily to others. A common saying in Haiti (with numerous variations) goes something like this: Haiti is 80 percent Christian and 100 percent Voodoo. "No, that's wrong," Joseph interrupted. "It's *110 percent* Voodoo."

There are several types of Christian responses to Voodoo. Some people, like Polycarpe Joseph, the Jesuit-trained Roman Catholic lay leader, recognize that Haiti is a spirit-filled place, where numerous traditions collide, intersect, and converge, and that many Catholics and not a few Protestants practice an element of this indigenous religion—it is as if it is in the air people breathe in Haiti. Indeed, the essence of Voodoo is its syncretic elements.

It combines the rich ritual elements of Catholicism and practices of African-influenced animism with a heavy emphasis on saints, deities, and magic, all overseen by what Voodoo practitioners believe is a supreme being. It has many of the same elements common to other religious practices in the Caribbean, such as Santeria in Cuba, which have combined elements of African religion and Roman Catholicism. "Syncretism doesn't bother me," Joseph told me, because it is so pervasive in Haiti. "When the Voodoo priests have their ceremonies, I laugh. They bother people in the neighborhoods with their loud drums—but pastors and priests do the same with their microphones and loudspeakers. All of them bother people in the neighborhoods."

Others place strict prohibitions on any intersection between Voodoo and Christianity. Garry Auguste, who helped me during the early days of my first assignment to Haiti, believes that the practice of Voodoo is devil's work and that such perceived evil can only be confronted by accepting Jesus into one's life. As a Pentecostal Christian, he is convinced that those in political power had gotten there at least partly thanks to a pact with evil spirits, with Voodoo. "Rulers get power the wrong way," said Auguste.

Immediately after the earthquake, the Rev. Pat Robertson, the U.S. evangelist and broadcast mogul, made a similar observation. During a January 13, 2010, broadcast on the Christian Broadcasting Network, he declared that Haitians "were under the heel of the French. You know, Napoleon III and whatever.... And they got together and swore a pact to the devil. They said, 'We will serve you if you will get us free from the French.' True story. And so, the devil said, 'Okay, it's a deal.'" Near-universal outrage greeted Robertson's remarks, which were condemned as insensitive, ahistorical, and un-Christian. Still, a number of Haitians expressed similar beliefs—from mild to robust. "God can do what he wants to do," one rural Haitian woman, Nana Fleristal, told me with assurance one morning outside a rural health clinic north of Port-au-Prince. "It could have been a punishment," she said of the earthquake. "We've done a lot of bad things. If God punished us, he wants us to know that he is the only God, and can do whatever he wants to on this earth." Whatever one feels about such comments, they do point to a truism: as elsewhere in the world but perhaps in an even deeper way, religion and spirituality in Haiti have always been deeply intertwined with social realities, economics, and politics.

An element of rebellion in the merger of faith traditions

Slavery accounts for much of that reality. The word *Voodoo* derives from West African vocabulary for "spirit" or "deity." As practiced in Haiti, it is tied to the historical memory of slaves who forged something new: a syncretic religion that combined African and European elements. Polycarpe Joseph believes there was an element of rebellion in this merger. Merging two religious realities—one African, one French-Catholic—made the combination something unique. Not wanting to fully emulate the Catholicism of their masters, the Haitian slaves "managed to add something and make it their own," he said. In doing so, the new religious practice placed great emphasis on serving the spirits. Many Voodoo ceremonies involve a *manbo*, a priestess, or *houngan*, a priest, preparing for possession—the way the spirit is said to enter a Voodoo believer.

The primacy of historical roots, ties to the land, and reverence of ancestors are important concepts in Voodoo, and has given Haitians a way of explaining the world. Voodoo gives them a sense of solace and power in the face of the heavy toils, burdens, and hardships of everyday life. When Haitians talk about Voodoo being "the soul" of their society, they are talking about the need to cope, to resist, and to find meaning in a brutal environment. As playwright and novelist Frank Etienne told Amy Wilentz, the Haitian peasant faces a "complicated system of exploitation designed to strip him of what little he is able to cultivate, what little land he owns. He has no access to justice. The practice of sorcery is his courtroom, his justice."

Different religious groups explain and deal with this reality in varying ways. In an interview with my coauthor Paul Jeffrey in early 2011, Yoleine Gateau, a Haitian human rights activist, said that a major problem for Haiti has been divisions sown by outsiders, like some U.S. Christians, who have seen Haiti, with its attendant poverty and hardship, as a natural destination for religious conversion. "Many religious groups come here because it's a poor country, and they offer people a bag of rice to convert. But that manner of conversion takes away any belief that you have in yourself, it takes away your soul. You'll believe whatever is necessary to get some more food from the foreigners," she said. One result, Gateau argued, is that it continues and exacerbates the long and difficult dynamic of Haitians' inability to unite around a common cause. Demonizing Voodoo can be part of that problem—which is why Gateau turns the use of the word *zombie*, someone who is placed under a trance by a Voodoo *bokor* or wizard, on its head. "Blaming Voodoo for everything bad that happens in Haiti has been a way for other religions to come in and turn people into zombies, taking their culture away and leaving them blank, with no sense of self-esteem," she said. "But who are you, and how can you accomplish anything, if you no longer believe in yourself? When you take away people's culture, what's left of you? Nothing. You become a zombie."

Certainly, Haitian evangelical Christians don't see it that way; many, like Nana Fleristal, who attends a Salvation Army congregation, say they are confident of God's power, based on a personal relationship they see in their own lives. Fleristal, for example, said she had no worries about Haiti's cholera epidemic. "Jesus Christ is already with me," she said, "so I don't have to worry about any sickness." Such confidence demonstrates the real inroads made in recent years by evangelical Protestants, particularly those from the U.S.

I asked Polycarpe Joseph why evangelical Protestantism, and particularly Pentecostalism, had taken such firm root. He believes a key reason is that the Catholic Church, despite pockets of progressive elements, had not shown sufficient "solidarity with the majority of the people." The rural poor saw Catholic clergy and female religious as "eating well, sleeping well," while the people themselves were living lives of deprivation. "There may be good priests, there may be good sisters," he said. "But you can't sleep well if one of the sheep can't sleep well."

On a Sunday afternoon, a gospel of personal piety

Belief in the primacy of a personal God was also in the air of Port-au-Prince on the Sunday before the first anniversary commemorations, during a widely advertised revival led by

Franklin Graham, son of American evangelist Billy Graham and the head of Samaritan's Purse, an organization that combines humanitarian relief and Christian evangelism. The group has often been criticized for combining these missions, particularly when it has used U.S. tax dollars for its assistance programs. Franklin Graham himself has garnered headlines and criticism for his condemnation of Islam—not a factor in Haiti, but nonetheless making him newsworthy. Given that record and the statements the Rev. Pat Robertson had made about Haiti, there was some curiosity about what Graham might say.

As it turned out, Graham offered little that was surprising or controversial. After an eclectic musical mix of singing Haitian Boy Scouts, Kreyòl Christian rap music, and American bluegrass, he delivered a stiff sermon to a full house, with several thousand people crowding into a downtown soccer stadium. Graham is not the spellbinding orator his father was during the height of his storied career—and people began getting restless and leaving the stadium about halfway through the thirty-minute oration.

Graham said he was in Haiti to remember the quake and its victims, to honor the survivors, and to pray that "God will cover you with his mercy." He expressed his belief that Haiti needed a "supernatural intervention," but that God loved Haiti. "We ask for His help and His guiding hand." Graham preached a gospel of personal piety, of new life and new beginnings, of a personal relationship with God. "He knows you," Graham said. "He knows everything about your life." He urged those who did not have a relationship with Jesus to declare publicly their desire to have one. "God is a God of great love. God is going to judge the world. And he will judge you one day. But he loves you. God is love." The only noticeable reaction to Graham's address came when he quoted a Haitian proverb that said it was all right to lie in order to get out of a tight spot. He also alluded to Voodoo when he said there are "those of you who worship other gods than the one God of heaven." People murmured in recognition.

While acknowledging injustices and grave suffering in the country, Graham made little reference to social problems in Haiti—either to the immediate problems of the slow pace of recovery since the earthquake or of sexual assaults on women in the camps, or longer-term problems, like economic and agricultural policies that had exerted painful costs on Haiti's poor majority. This was probably not surprising—it represented the tenor of the times. One long-time U.S. aid worker recalled that during the 1970s and 1980s, the Roman Catholic Church in Haiti began to shed some of its traditional conservatism and began speaking out for the poor majority. When he was a priest, Father Aristide brought some of that fire to the debate. For example, his condemnation that U.S. money and food assistance were impediments in Haiti: "The money helps to maintain an armed force against the people; the food helps to ruin our national economy; and both money and food keep Haiti in a situation of dependence on the former colonizers." Of course, even in those earlier, tumultuous times, Aristide's was a distinctly minority voice among Catholic clergy. But even so, this aid worker observed, "The Catholic Church today is largely absent as a progressive voice."

Still, if we define the church in a broader context, the movements for change are not lying dormant. The history of outright repression and violence over the last three decades has led to the formation of grassroots organizations opting to attack Haiti's problems in concrete ways, often dealing with specific problems, like discrimination against women, or the problems of hunger. There are dozens of these groups in Port-au-Prince. Most of them take a pragmatic approach, with an occasional nod to the past, like hanging a portrait of revolutionary Ernesto "Che" Guevera on an office wall. (More than forty years after his death, Guevera remains a potent symbol of rebellion and resistance throughout the Caribbean and Latin America.) Yet for all their pragmatism, the mission of these organizations, with historic roots in the "popular church," remains progressive and is undergirded by the ideas and language of liberation theology—the belief that God is on the side of the poor.

The continued influence of liberation theology

In speaking passionately about the food cooperatives, Cher-Frere Fortune's boss, the Rev. Herode Guillomettre, speaks of the poor and nonpoor working together for greater dignity for all Haitians, and of the need to cooperate, especially in the light of Haiti's postearthquake reality. He rejects the label of a wholly progressive theology. Instead, he embraces what he calls "integrative theology," which includes elements of liberation theology's social emphasis, but adds ingredients of "soul, body, and spirit. The spirit needs food, the body needs food, the soul needs food," he said. "We try to see the entire person in a holistic way." In defining his approach to church as "integrated," he said, "it takes the good parts of all different theologies, not just liberation theology, and emphasizes Jesus' call to solidarity, love, justice, and participation." I asked how he would explain this to the outside world—for instance, to U.S. churches desiring to support Haiti, but not sure exactly how to do so. "We need to advocate for a new Haiti, and for that we need the church to stand up for Haiti, not to abandon it. But churches must support the calls to strengthen Haitian's voice at the table. Because I can tell you right now, they (Haitians) don't have that ownership now"—a reference to the fact that many Haitians felt they had been left out of major decisions about how relief and reconstruction funds were to be dispersed, continuing unfair and unjust neocolonial dynamics.

"Haiti was already in the midst of many other earthquakes"

The several mornings I spent with Polycarpe Joseph were at the Ecumenical Foundation for Peace and Justice, which among other tasks, sponsors and runs an educational training program for young people in Port-au-Prince. When I asked Joseph about the evocations of liberation theology suggested by some of the things I heard him say, he smiled. While sitting in a simple office, devoid of any decoration and anchored by a nearly empty desk, he elaborated on his theological stance. "There's no better way to serve God than by serving others. If you want to meet God, you have to meet God in others' suffering." Particularly the poor. "We believe Jesus came for everybody but especially the poor." That belief is the foundation for Joseph's organization: "We believe in action and results. An action that doesn't end in a result isn't worth it."

He rattled off the communities his organization had worked with: with young people who were caught in waves of repression that followed the 1994 coup; with emigrants who had been sent back from Guantanamo Bay, Cuba, following failed attempts to enter the

United States; with children and youths known as "restaveks" who essentially work as slaves in urban households; with urban gangs in Port-au-Prince.

"We think that before the 2010 earthquake, Haiti was already in the midst of many other earthquakes: the people's social conditions were an earthquake, as was their increasing misery," Joseph said. "People were not living as humans, laws were not being respected, the majority of people were not able to eat. God is not indifferent to that, and since God is not indifferent to that, people can't be indifferent to that. That's true of the church as well. A church that is not engaged with the poor is not a church. A church that does not recognize the suffering of the hungry is a not a church. A church that does not recognize the problems of the poor is not a church. A real church has to be in touch with the cries of the people."

He paused. "Poverty and misery are all theological questions, as are questions of peace and development. We can't have peace without development and development without peace—and when I talk of development I mean education, jobs, putting hunger behind us. That is the development we are looking for. In the past year, we've become theologians in action, because all of the crumbling foundations have taken us—clergy, laity, NGO workers—into the camps, into the streets. That moment of the quake was not the moment to have us all kneel down in prayer, but to save people in the rubble. We acted. It became incarnational."

Recalling a comment made by Rabbi Brent Spodek of American Jewish World Service, that it is human nature to ask why "God caused the earth to shudder," I asked Joseph the theodicy question. For an instant, he looked annoyed. But then he looked at me evenly. "An earthquake doesn't have to do with God's punishment; it's a natural phenomenon," he said. "It makes me very sad that some pastors have said this—this idea of divine punishment. The problem with Haiti was that most people died because buildings collapsed," he said, echoing what Spodek had said about what was the truly productive question: what were we "doing on January 11—and the days, months and years before that—when Haiti was already the poorest country in the Western Hemisphere?" The *extent* of the tragedy was due to human neglect and to the Haiti that existed prior to January 12, 2010, not to divine punishment. "Our God is a loving God, not a vindictive God," Joseph said. "God is not here to punish an entire country."

Is Haiti Hopeless?

Inevitably, anyone who has lived or worked in Haiti for any length of time is bound to be asked if Haiti is hopeless. One of the many people who have asked me that was a family friend who had donated to one of the many Haitian causes in 2010—in his case, a humanitarian group focusing on water purification. He wondered if, in the end, his contribution—*anyone's* contribution—had done any good, made any impact.

I told him that if he trusted and knew that the group did solid work, there was a good chance the contribution had done some good, though the humanitarian response in Haiti is, as we've seen, marked by extreme difficulties, and that a certain level of imperfection of work has to be expected by donors giving to any humanitarian operation. That's the reality of humanitarianism. But as to whether Haiti is hopeless, I replied no: to simply write off Haiti as a place beyond all hope—as a country of humans without agency, where change is, and will *never* be, possible—is deeply unfair to Haiti, and to Haitians. I've worked alongside too many Haitians to believe otherwise. "If you say Haiti is hopeless, it's like you're saying that Haitians aren't even people," Finnish aid worker Sylvia Raulo told me.

The suggestion also goes up against the evidence of recent global history. In my lifetime, there are any number of countries and regions once thought to be immovable and unchangeable—the Soviet Union, Eastern Europe—that have indeed undergone substantial transformations. And as I write this, the Middle East is reeling from an "Arab Spring," in which the cries for change have been keenly felt and heard, catching the world off-guard. Yet the situation in Egypt is telling: a government can be overthrown, but the painful realities of day-to-day governing, reform, and substantive change are still to come. Those type of hard realities resonate in Haiti, where, since the 1990s, a succession of governments have had very limited room in which to maneuver, given the pressures of neoliberal policies that made it virtually impossible for Haiti to control its destiny. Complaints by Haitians about the government's impotence and inability to do much, perhaps best symbolized by the continued presence of UN peacekeeping forces in a country not experiencing a civil conflict, should hardly come as a surprise. Haiti, as Peter

Hallward notes, is a place where "increased reliance on foreign aid, increased penetration of the economy by foreign NGOs, increased international supervision of the national police" has become the norm. In such an environment, even the modest attempts, such as Aristide's, to "move from abject misery to a semi-dignified poverty," as Hallward put it, have been impossible.

And then there was the earthquake, an event that had its equivalent occurred in the United States, it could have shaken institutions, certainly the federal government, to the core. "What would our own government be like if it had faced the same situation?" mused Robert Radtke, president of Episcopal Relief & Development, the humanitarian arm of the U.S. Episcopal Church. "What if one-quarter of the population had in some way been affected, the centers of government and media had been destroyed, the president was forced into a bunker. Then, we're essentially invaded by foreign powers. The Chinese fly into Ottawa to come across the Canadian border, reinstate 'order' and tell us how to run our country. Spin it out in our context and it looks like a catastrophe." It does, and it would for any country, but particularly a country as institutionally weakened as Haiti. But does that mean change is impossible *in* Haiti?

It certainly does no one any good to gloss over Haiti's problems, both internal and external, by simply reiterating the mantra of "hope." Haiti *is* a tough, complex, difficult place "where things don't happen quickly," said Melissa Crutchfield of the United Methodist Committee on Relief. Similarly, Pix Mahler, a Presbyterian missionary with years of experience in Haiti, knows North Americans can express exasperation, impatience, and frustration over Haiti—its logistical challenges, its corruption, its seemingly overwhelming and intractable problems. At times, a country that is only six hundred miles from the southern coast of the United States can seem "almost as if it's from a different cosmos."

Haiti does have its own realities. In her rhapsodic, beautifully woven, and yet ultimately devastating short story *Claire of the Sea Light*, Edwidge Danticat stares down Haiti's social realities: widowed fathers leave their daughters so they can start new lives; children die too young; impoverished fishermen are lost in an instant due to a "rogue wave." But Danticat writes of these realities in a sublimely humane way, beyond the traditional frames of pity and remorse. That, of course, is the particular power of stories, but fiction's gift of empathy and insight has implications in other spheres: in the realm of advocacy and enlightened policy, in the place where politics and citizen response overlap.

"A missed opportunity to empower Haitians"

During Holy Week of 2011, people I met on previous assignments—including Polycarpe Joseph and Herode Guillomettre, president of the Christian Center for Integrated Development—said candidly that the chance to substantially change Haiti's course after the earthquake had probably been lost. Guillomettre said, "It was a missed opportunity to empower Haitians." And why was such an opening squandered? Because old patterns reemerged: outside NGOs gained power, leaving Haitians with little place at the table. Joseph said while he was not yet 100 percent discouraged, he was disappointed. In the days and weeks immediately following the quake, he recalled, "The energy was extraordinary, and for the first three months, we needed that, we needed the help of the international NGOs." However, soon after that, something could have been done "to launch something new. But we lost that opportunity because, by that point, we had lost our sovereignty. The Haitian authorities should have taken charge. But they didn't. When I saw that onslaught of NGOs, I knew that there would be no development."

By "development," Joseph meant what he and Guillomettre and others had long advocated: not top-heavy projects dictated from outside, but smaller-scale undertakings, developed by Haitians, that could ultimately spin off and become self-sustaining, so that *Haitians could become self-sufficient*. For example, the food cooperatives may not be a panacea for all that ails Haiti, but as small-scale work that had achieved self-sufficiency and had given its members a measure of food security, it seemed to have worked. That was one demonstration of Haiti's promise.

Another plan of action showed both the strength and limitations of Haiti's current realities. One of the cornerstone programs of Polycarpe Joseph's Ecumenical Center for Peace and Justice is an initiative to provide education for children and young people at risk, including former gang members, teenage mothers, and "restaveks"—children forced into unpaid domestic servitude. The center's original building was destroyed in the quake, but thanks to support from U.S. churches, the center quickly revived and reopened its doors in late 2010. The training of cooks, hairdressers, and mechanics in a comfortable, airy space in Port-au-Prince's Carrefour-feuilles neighborhood is impressive.

So are its students. One of them, twenty-two-year-old Mikency Jean, a native of Cap Haitian, came to Port-au-Prince at age eleven to work as a restavek for her aunt. Jean's real dream has been to become a nurse. But that dream is beyond her reach because she does not have the money to study nursing. She has, however, been able to save enough money to take cooking classes and training at the center, where students pay only a small fee. "Any day I don't go to the center, I feel awful," she said. Jean's specialty and love is making salads—she wants to work at a restaurant someday. While she dreams of a better life, she says that she and others her age are skittish about the future. Why? They are not sure if their training will get them the jobs they want. "We talk about it all the time," she said, "and we don't feel there is a bright future for the country."

Policies can change

It is that pessimism that Haitian leaders like Joseph and Guillomettre want to combat, and it is why they constantly say that they need allies—like the faith community, grassroots groups, human rights activists—to make the case for better trade, agricultural, and aid policies in Washington and other world capitals. Despite the many frustrations since January 2010, can that happen? It happened when faith-based groups, among others, championed the cause of Haiti debt relief following the quake, arguing that canceling Haiti's outstanding $1 billion external debt could help Haiti in its recovery and reconstruction efforts. International grass-roots campaigning paid off. By July 2010, Inter-American Development Bank, the International Monetary Fund and the World Bank agreed to cancel the debts Haiti owed the agencies.

More broadly, long-time antihunger advocate David Beckmann of Bread for the World has argued that global antipoverty policies *can* change—that the tireless, even unrelenting, efforts of advocates have paid off with real results. Those at the grassroots, Beckmann writes in *Exodus from Hunger: We Are Called to Change the Politics of Hunger*, "can often sway Congress to make changes that help millions of hungry people."

One example is a new antihunger initiative by the Obama administration that has not received much attention beyond the world of humanitarian and development work. The new policy direction, called "Feed the Future," takes into account what advocacy groups have been saying for years: that globally U.S. development policy needs to provide more pronounced support for small, poor farmers—like those in Haiti—hoping to boost the production of their crops so that they can better feed their families and communities. Other initiatives are focusing on the concern of Dr. Marius and other Haitians: the need to do something for undernourished children, including the interventions against undernutrition during the first one thousand days of pregnancy and childhood. This new emphasis and direction as policy just didn't happen magically—it happened because Bread for the World and supporters of other advocacy and humanitarian groups understood change was needed and made a case that it was good for U.S. policy.

Haitians' need for allies is tempered by the realization that Haitians must constantly remind friends of Haiti of what is at stake. Aid has poured into Haiti not only since 2010, but also during years before the catastrophe—and yet, as Guillomettre argues, the issue of sustainability is still not emphasized enough. "We need to support a vision of the Haitian people where they can be actors in their own development and stop the cycle of dependency," he said. "You can't have tent cities forever."

That is true. On a Sunday morning in January 2011, in a windswept area north of Port-au-Prince, Calvin Bourre, a resident of a relatively new displacement area, the Corail camp, told me he wants to leave the earthquake behind. But he can't. The twenty-four-year-old son of a Pentecostal pastor spoke of setbacks and fears—losing work and his home, worries about his children getting sick, uncertainty about the future. In his current life, he called himself "so far from that 'godly light,'" adding, "but it's not me, it's Haiti. It's everywhere. Haiti doesn't want you to be anybody." Sometimes, he says, "I start dreaming hard. I feel ashamed. It's not a life. It's not a life. It's not a life at all." There are days he doesn't leave the house. "The kids cry. I say, 'Daddy don't got it. Daddy don't got it.'"

Bourre had been at Corail since April, and in a house—what is often called "transitional housing"—for about a month. In contrast to the tent cities, it's not a bad place. The camp has wider spaces, important for a small family with young children. The problem is that Corail is so far from Port-au-Prince. Bourre is a construction and repair worker, who once worked regularly in the city. But now, given his distance from Port-au-Prince, he must make do with cash-for-work programs at the camp that are off-and-on: two to three weeks of work, then long stretches with nothing.

I asked Bourre how long he expects to be at Corail. "I think it's going to be forever," he said. "They did good for us, as far as this house," he said. But he still worries about money, family, and work.

Bourre has worked for change. He was a leader of protests at the camp in September 2010 aimed at getting people out of the tents and into something better. "It did have an effect. Two weeks later, they started to move on things." In a limited way, that showed the continued power of the streets, something more recognizable with the election of a new president.

A new president—renewed optimism and old worries

Though elected with less than 25 percent of eligible voters casting their ballot, and with the leftist Lavalas party banned from participating in the election, Michel Martelly, a one-time Carnival singer known as "Sweet Micky," took office in May 2011 with promises of a new beginning, unburdened by traditional politics or politicians. In particular, he pledged expansion of educational opportunities to be funded by, among other things, a tax on lottery tickets. As Polycarpe Joseph tartly pointed out, "For two hundred years, the elite has known that people need to read and write," he said, "but they have not done anything to provide that. They could have done this a long time ago and did not."

In the month before his inaugural in May 2011, there seemed to be general good will toward Martelly, particularly among young people. However, the optimism was tempered by fear that the cycle of corrupt politics would once again consume and cripple another president. "They try to change the system, but it's the system that changes them," Joseph said. "Look at Aristide. The system ate him. It's the way the system is built. Your hands are tied."

There are good reasons to be cautious. As Mark Danner pointed out in 1989, Haitians "speak wryly of *le Fauteuil*—the Chair":

> Every Haitian of note seems to want the Chair, but once he has taken his place in it the Chair imprisons him and transforms him. The mumbling country doctor becomes a ferocious monster, the stuttering general becomes a drunken Caligula. For, once in the Chair, the Haitian ruler -- "provisional" or permanent, king or general -- finds himself with no choice but to fight to keep it. It was in this fight, in his determination to endure, that Francois Duvalier revealed his genius, by fashioning a repressive system that persists to this day. "All these candidates and their pronouncements are a joke," one of his followers told me proudly not long ago. "Duvalier still rules this land. He will rule it for fifty years."

The most pernicious effects of the first Duvalier regime may have worn off a bit sooner than fifty years (though probably not nearly enough), and the good will toward Martelly was palpable in early 2011. But Haitians have enough experience with politicians—and know enough of the outside constraints, machinations, and pressures (e.g., from the U.S.) that constantly face them—to be wisely weary of easy promises. "I don't know what he can do," Saint Soit Joseph, fifty-three, a Port-au-Prince laborer and mason, said of Martelly when he and I spoke the day after Easter 2011 in the *Cité Soleil* area of Port-au-Prince. "But we can hope."

Ironically, some of that hope is based on nostalgia for the very political figure Martelly, who is sometimes called a neo-Duvalierist for his past relationships with anti-Aristide political figures (some with poor human rights records), has professed to dislike. The nostalgia for Aristide seems to be most alive for those living on or close to the streets.

"When they're elected, they promise a lot"

Some people, including Guillomettre, didn't vote in the spring 2011 presidential election in protest, saying the election was little more than show for the international community. He said the $30 million spent on the election would have been better spent on earthquake recovery efforts. Others voted but were not particularly hopeful. "We're not sure what it means yet," said twenty-six-year-old Anne Suze Denestant, who lost her right arm in the quake. When I first met her in January 2011, she expressed exasperation that so little had been done by Haitian authorities in the previous year. "It's a wait-and-see time for us. When they're elected, they promise a lot." She had a similar reaction to the preelection return of Aristide, someone her parents had supported, saying his return "doesn't mean anything to me."

Polycarpe Joseph and Herode Guillomettre said they thought Aristide's return could lead to some reconciliation in the country as it tried to recover from the quake and years of political turmoil. But while neither man admired the new president—Guillomettre compared Martelly to rock star Alice Cooper and chided him for promotion of what he called a debased culture—both seemed delighted that Martelly had upended traditional politics and had given the Haitian elite something of a drubbing. "It's a lesson to the politicians," Guillomettre told me. "They need to be closer to the people, have their feet on the ground, and need to know the realities of the country."

Who has power in Haiti?

That lesson to Haiti's elite is tied up with a dynamic underlying politics and social realities anywhere but has particular resonance in a country where the constant jockeying for domination is something of a sport—the question of power. Who actually has power in Haiti? Certainly, the elite, the United States government, NGOs, the United Nations all have power, and will continue to have and use that power in the years to come. Joseph, among others, believes that the earthquake may have led to a dispersal of power. Yes, outside powers like the United States continue to have dominating power. "They are in charge," he said. But Martelly's election means that there is still some power among the poor—though "whenever the population stands up, the elites will always try to get that back." True enough, said Herode Guillomettre, but Martelly's election was proof, in a limited way, he said, "that power can still be in the streets. There can still be a power of resistance."

There is also the power of patience—something that Presbyterian missionary Pix Mahler counsels when she says "patience, patience, prayer, and more patience" are needed when U.S. citizens approach Haiti's difficulties. She cautions those who think they have the answers to the country's problems to think about this: "Haiti is a gift to us. If we have the patience and time to look at those differences, we can appreciate Haiti rather than feeling *we* have all of the answers and that only *we* can give to Haiti. Haiti has been and continues to be an epiphany, an opportunity to carry out God's mission—to not only give, but to *receive* the gift of relationship and sensitivity." Mahler said she "shudders" with delight in thinking of Haiti's many potentials—its hardworking people, for one. Without minimizing the challenges ahead, she remains optimistic about Haiti's long-term promise.

Others, it has to be acknowledged, take a far dimmer view—not because of any lack of promise in Haitians but because of the current state of the world and Haiti's particular place in it. Writer Junot Díaz argues that the Haitian earthquake revealed not only Haiti *itself* but something of our entire world and current global system—and the view is damning. "Look closely into the apocalypse of Haiti," Díaz wrote in a 2011 essay, "and you will see that Haiti's problem is not that it is poor and vulnerable—Haiti's problem is that it is poor and vulnerable at a time in our capitalist experiment when the gap between those who got grub and those who don't is not only vast but also rapidly increasing. Said another way, Haiti's nightmarish vulnerability has to be understood as part of a larger trend of *global inequality*." In Haiti, we see possible portents of a future where some countries may never see *any* benefits from what Díaz calls the world's "new, rapacious stage of capitalism." Their future? Bleak doesn't even begin to describe it. We have entered a stage of history, Díaz argues, "where, in order to power the explosion of the super-rich and the ultra-rich, middle classes are being forced to fail, working classes are being re-proletarianized, and the poorest are being pushed beyond the grim limits of subsistence, into a kind of sepulchral half-life, perfect targets for any 'natural disaster' that just happens to wander by."

A point of pride for African people throughout the world

That is a bleak view—and even Diaz tempers it by arguing that "apocalypses like the Haitian earthquake are not only catastrophes; they are also opportunities: chances for us to see ourselves, to take responsibility for what we see, to change." One needed change has been offered by African-American historian Mahmoud El-Kati, who believes it is time to challenge what he called the "prevailing, one dimensional, simplistic view" of Haiti that "normalizes the image of Haiti as only a place of social death." Buried beneath the rubble, El-Kati argues, is the fact that Haiti once destroyed what he called the governing myth of the modern world—that of white supremacy—and that it continues to stand "as a beacon of hope, a source of inspiration, and pride for African people throughout the modern world." Haiti's triumphant past, he argues, "is greater than its present reality."

So, too, is the potential of its people.

Louis Dorvilier, who succeeded Sylvia Raulo as the representative of the Lutheran World Federation in Haiti, left a job with the Evangelical Lutheran Church in America in Chicago to return to his native country in late 2010. Like other Haitians, Dorvilier has felt the sting of frustration about the slow pace of overall reconstruction work and by often overlapping and uncoordinated humanitarian efforts.

But Dorvilier said he remains hopeful that if Haitians can yet be given the opportunity to drive and lead rebuilding and reconstruction efforts, a new country can emerge. While the efforts of humanitarian groups can only "fill in gaps," he believes that Haiti must look toward building wealth and developing a middle class. "I don't think the Salvation Army, or the Lutherans or the Methodists can do that by themselves."

What religious bodies and institutions *can* do is see and affirm a larger picture—a universal story of struggle and resistance, of pain and promise. Dorvilier finds particular resonance in the Gospel of Matthew's Christmas narrative of the Holy Family's flight to Egypt. Like Haitians after the earthquake, "Jesus and his family were on the move; they were tenting out, camping out." In that sense, the view of the biblical stories from the perspective of Haitians today, he said, is "very incarnational. It's also a theology of grace: despite all of the challenges the people of this country face, the Haitian people believe that God is with them, that God is caring for them, that God is living with them." Dorvilier paused. "People have asked me, why I am going to a place where there is cholera, hurricanes, earthquakes," he said. "My answer is that Haiti remains one of the most incredible places on earth… the potential for an expanded economy stirs in me a great sense of call. I'm here to work with the Haitian people. Hope is here," he said. "It's why we are all still alive. It's only because of God's grace. We need to celebrate that."

Postscript

During Holy Week 2011, I retraced some of my steps from previous assignments. I returned to Sister Marcella's clinic. Sister Marcella was away on holiday, but I was told cholera cases were on the increase again: more than a dozen people were laid out on cots, saline bags next to them. But among those I spoke to, there also appeared to be measured hope for the new president, particularly among those who once supported Aristide. "Aristide was the only president who cared about the poor," said saleswoman Doudeline Surena. "We don't know if Martelly will be that way. But we certainly hope so."

I went to see Calvin Bourre at the ever-expanding Corail camp and saw signs of permanence creeping in. Many homes, including Bourre's, were freshly painted and many had plants and gardens in front. Bourre was not at home—but his girlfriend and neighbors told me he still had not found work. Neighbor August Paulerel was more upbeat about the situation at the camp than Bourre had been earlier in the year. Paulerel, who had lived at the camp for a year, admitted the job situation remained difficult—he had only found sporadic work as a day laborer at the camp. However, he liked the result of the election, finding some hope in Michel Martelly's election. And the return of Aristide was a signal that the former president still had concern for people like him. "Any kind of government is corrupt, but the others were worse. Aristide was still the only president who cared about the poor."

On Easter Sunday, I attended an early morning service at Rev. Guillomettre's church, where Pentecostal and Baptist traditions co-mingle; he told me the service would be "hot"—and it was. He preached passionately about the living God, of Jesus no longer being in the tomb, of a personal and social God. "God has a plan for each of you. The Gospel has a power to change you. Stand near that cross." But he also said: "God needs me to preach a Gospel which is related with the reality we are living now."

Later that morning, I met some congregants who attended Easter services at Holy Trinity Episcopal Cathedral in downtown Port-au-Prince, which had been nearly destroyed in the earthquake. While it would take years to rebuild the cathedral, the pain over the physical loss of the cathedral—including a school and all but three of the cathedral's famed fourteen murals painted by revered Haitian artists—had begun to diminish, they said. The resilience of the congregation itself is what matters the most, said long-time member Romilus Jean Dieudoné, seventy-five. "We are the church, not the building," he said, placing his hand over his heart. "And today is the day of rebirth." Another long-time congregant, Madame Nicolas Canier, sixty-two, agreed. "Jesus Christ has taken victory on this day." A younger member said people were tired of discussing the quake and its aftermath. "We can't take in any more of the negative stuff," said thirty-year-old Victor Nickenson. "The earthquake is something in the past. We need to think of the new life, the life ahead."

✦　　　✦　　　✦

Afterword:
A New Solidarity with Haiti

By Paul Jeffrey

The Haitian earthquake generated a new word in the vocabulary of Haitians: *goudougoudou*. It's the slightly affectionate Kreyòl term that Haitians across the board use to name the disaster that ravaged Port-au-Prince and nearby cities in 2010. It's alternately written *goudou goudou* or *goudou-goudou*, and is supposedly—if you say it over and over again very fast—the sound that the buildings made as they swayed and collapsed during the quake. More than just a word for an event, however, it's a playful invention used by people of all social classes and religious orientations to name something so horrible that it's better to call it something else, even if they had to make up a name. Linguists call this an *onomatopoeia*, naming something for the sound it makes. I suspect it also has psychosocial value in that it restores some sense of power to people who were made to feel powerless in those thirty-some seconds of terror. Naming, after all, was one of the first powers that God bestowed on humanity in the Genesis narratives, and naming the quake is a way for Haitians of turning back toward paradise from the fallen state in which they dwell today.

That they invented such a word tells me a lot about Haitians. Nowhere else can you find a people who have so repeatedly gotten the short end of the stick from empires and economies, yet they keep about themselves a joy for life that is infectious and endearing. As a journalist, I cover a lot of desperate situations, yet seldom do I find a people who, although trampled upon repeatedly, refuse, in general, to be victims.

I had made several trips to Haiti before the quake and been emotionally marked by its extreme poverty. If there ever was a poster child for the vulnerability which is the prime ingredient of disaster, it was Haiti. It's that vulnerability that made the disaster—forget the word "natural"—a direct result of the country's legacy of exploitation. That long chain of Haitian history begins with import of slaves during French colonial control and passes through the high price of Haitian independence and through the long decades of U.S. gunboat diplomacy, when we kept Haiti at an arm's length lest its rebellious spirit infect black slaves in the U.S. South. In more recent times, the Clinton and Bush administrations did all they could to undermine the work of Haiti's first democratically elected president, Jean-Bertrand Aristide, and then lied masterfully about it in order to make Aristide look like the villain. That effectively kept others in the hemisphere from being inspired by this potent example of liberation theology made flesh. This history explains much about Haiti today, and ignorance of it will lead us quickly down the road to misunderstanding and paternalism.

More than a year after the quake, I hear people in the U.S. ask why it's taking so long to "rebuild" Haiti. The problem with that question is that it assumes the problem began on

January 12, 2010. Yet Haiti wasn't just a disaster "waiting to happen" before the quake, it was already a full-fledged disaster. So to rebuild the capital and its environs today, we must wrestle with an international context that has conspired to keep Haitians oppressed and working cheaply. We must come to terms with how our country's foreign policy toward Haiti was most succinctly summed up by the officer who led the Marines ashore in 1915 at the beginning of a two-decade-long occupation. "I know the nigger and how to handle him," Colonel Littleton Waller said. Unless we start to understand how Colonel Waller's racism continues to poison Haiti's future, the democratic spring that Aristide envisioned will remain deferred, and reconstruction from the quake will simply not happen.

Many who will read this book participate in denominations or faith communities in the U.S. that frequently send "mission teams" to Haiti. Just as our country's political policies toward Haiti have often born bad fruit, so have our religious practices at times contributed to the disempowerment of Haitians. As we struggle with our political complicity, we should also ask hard questions about mission policies and practices that reinforce paternalism, encourage dependency, and strive to alienate Haitians from their own rich culture. Otherwise we just serve as useful fools for the Haitian oligarchy, a small group that has never cared much for the poor. That's why they've done so little to provide education or health services, for example, while encouraging foreigners to come and build schools and orphanages and clinics that serve to tamper down dissent and remove social agency from the poor, all the while letting the rich off the hook. The resultant culture of dependency, in what some have come to call the "Republic of NGOs," has been devastating to the Haitian spirit.

So our mission in Haiti, if it is to be truly God's mission, must be something other than religious tourism masquerading as development aid. I have seen vans of mission volunteers driving past the tent cities in Port-au-Prince, the white faces staring out the windows at what must appear to them to be appalling poverty. What they would realize, if they'd get off the bus and spend time listening to real Haitians, is that they're real people—with joys and foibles and hopes and dreams—who are much more complex than any two-dimensional view of them as helpless victims who need rescuing.

The images I have chosen for this book are my humble attempt to begin to offer a visual look at how complex a place Haiti is. Yes, it's poor, at least most of it, but there's a dignity that often transforms victims into survivors, that in the best of times makes Haitians the subject of their own history rather than the object of someone else's.

As a photographer, there are times when I inevitably end up intruding on people's lives. Yet in Haiti I have been repeatedly welcomed with hospitality and humor, even though I may be just one more *blanc* poking around in their lives. It can be a complex encounter, yet one that exhibits the impishness, creativity, compassion, and strength of many Haitians. For example, I can be walking around a Port-au-Prince slum capturing images of the everyday life of some of the eight hundred thousand people who remain living in what are generously called tents. Upon seeing me, a Haitian will sometimes rub his or her stomach and say, *Mwen grangou*—"I'm hungry." They want me to give them some money. I don't do that. I'll often explain that I'm a journalist, or (depending on the setting) that I work with an aid group working in the camp, and that I'm there to document what's happening so that people in the rest of the world will know what they're living through. My translator does this rap in Kreyòl a lot of the time without me initiating it. And I'll often use the opening provided by their statement to ask them how they're getting along.

What I find fascinating is the change that comes over people once they realize they're not getting anything directly from me. A person who one minute is trying really hard to look pitiful and hungry will return to looking dignified, smile, and maybe even give me a thumbs-up or a fist bump. This isn't to argue that they are not hungry. They very well may be. Life in the camps is harder than ever, and I've watched mothers feed their children biscuits made from dirt, lard, and salt because it's the only thing they can afford. But there's a mask they often put on in this encounter, a disguise which has long worked with the *blancs* who flock here to do things for them. If it hadn't worked in the past, they wouldn't keep doing it. In essence, we've made them perform like victims in order for us to happily disburse our largesse in a way that allows us to feel like heroes but really changes nothing in the long run. Yet when Haitians are treated as normal people rather than objects of pity, they straighten up and are often happy to talk about their lives, including what happened to them and their loved ones during the *goudougoudou*.

Rebuilding Haiti means treating Haitians as adults. They are capable of developing their country socially and economically, and we certainly can help with that. But a new relationship is necessary, one of partnership and solidarity, to replace the long disaster of recent Haitian history.

Interview with Chris Herlinger and Paul Jeffrey

This is your second book together. How did you come to collaborate?

Chris: Paul and I have collaborated before, particularly on various assignments for ACT Alliance. In addition, we've both won Catholic Relief Services' Egan Award and traveled with CRS twice together in the Middle East. So we're not strangers. As for the books, Davis Perkins of Church Publishing had seen photographs and reporting from Darfur that Paul had done for *The Christian Century* and asked him if he was interested in doing a book. Paul said he didn't have time to do the text, so I was invited in on the project. As for this book, the project took shape after Paul and I had both worked together and separately in Haiti. As we found ourselves going back to Haiti a few times, the idea of a book seemed pretty logical.

You both have been to some of the most troubled places on earth and met people suffering in desperate situations. How have these experiences affected you both professionally and personally?

Paul: If suffering is accidental, it's tragic and can produce sympathy and sadness. But when it's a product of injustice and greed, it produces anger, motivating me to work to change the situation of injustice.

It's important to note, however, that no matter the level of suffering, I'm constantly surprised and amazed by the grace of people who refuse to be victims. Instead, they are survivors, and they often offer me, a stranger, a gift of hospitality and grace. The poorer they are, the more likely they are to recover quickly from disasters. Despair, it seems, is a privilege of class.

Chris: One thing to keep in mind: we're working for humanitarian agencies, so we're not hard-core "front-line" war guys. Still, having said that—yes, we've seen our share of suffering. I can only speak for myself, but the people I've met have had amazing capacities to survive and overcome adversity. They're the real heroes in these situations, and their examples of endurance are the real stories. We're just the storytellers, and I'd rather keep the focus off us. I get uncomfortable when the focus is *on* us.

How soon did you arrive in Haiti after the earthquake? What were your immediate impressions of postquake Port-au-Prince?

Chris: Paul arrived about a week before I did; I arrived about two weeks after the quake. We were based in Pétionville, a suburb of Port-au-Prince, and an area not as badly hit as others. So actually my immediate impressions were not overwhelming. But that all changed within a day, after seeing the damage of downtown Port-au-Prince, which *was* overwhelming. It's a cliché, but I had never seen anything like it.

Chris, as a journalist how do you balance being "on the job" with being a witness to almost unbearable human suffering?

A musician I admire compared a performance to being in a funnel, and that's not a bad analogy for being a humanitarian journalist. When you're on assignment, working in a situation like Haiti, you're just incredibly focused on seeing things, taking it all in, talking to people, trying to get stories, balancing what your colleagues back home need right away versus what can wait for a longer article or even a book. There is a lot of shaping of ideas, and certainly there is a lot more awareness now of getting stories for different uses—longer pieces, social media. But as you're doing all of this, you're just focused, focused, focused.

You have to bring a certain amount of objectivity to the work—that doesn't mean you can't be an empathetic human being. In fact, that has to be the basis for what you're doing; otherwise, what's the point? You're there to tell stories. But you have to be continually thinking of what you need, who you need to talk to—are you talking to a wide range of people, women, young people, elderly? There are lots of questions in your mind as you're doing your work. Maybe that sounds clinical, but being "on the job" actually keeps you sane. Being "on the job" allows you to witness better. You feel with your eyes, see with your heart.

As the writer, I think I have it easier than the photographer. I know this from working with Paul so many times, but it bears repeating: in places like Haiti or in Africa, where the sun is so intense during the middle of the day, there are really only two times a day where you get the quality of light you want for really good photographs: early morning and late afternoon. So a photographer has to be even more focused. A writer can get a great quote in the middle of the night. It's much, much harder to get a great photo at midnight.

Paul, in her book, *On Photography*, Susan Sontag wrote, "To photograph is to appropriate the thing photographed. It means putting oneself into a certain relation to the world that feels like knowledge—and, therefore, like power." How do you respond to that statement in terms of your own work in Haiti?

It's true that images provide a strong way of knowing a place or a people or a particular situation, yet I feel more privileged than powerful as a photographer, privileged to be allowed into the lives of people and communities and then to share what I see through the lens with others.

Stories of mass murder, calamitous natural events, and massive national corruption can be so overwhelming that observers, even the most sympathetic, turn away because it is almost impossible to even think about such events and situations, let alone understand them. How do you envision your books bridging that divide?

Paul: You left out massive *international* corruption, certainly a major factor in Haiti's injustice. Hopefully the readers of this book will come away with a greater understanding of that.

But in terms of how we can help readers overcome feelings of wanting to flee from pain and conflict, the key may be to think small and local. In my book *Recovering Memory*, about the peace process in Guatemala, I focused on how ordinary people often did extraordinary things in the midst of that country's genocidal violence. That's precisely how to help people understand difficult historical moments. Statistics and analysis often are numbing, something psychologist Paul Slovic has convincingly documented, but narratives of how particular people suffer, or alternately carve out spaces for life in the midst of overwhelming violence, can invite the reader into understanding history in a very accessible way.

What single encounter or image is most emblematic of your experience of Haiti?

Paul: A very personal anecdote: several years ago I was walking around alone, shooting in Cité Soleil, one of the poorest neighborhoods anywhere, when it started raining. The streets flooded and yet I continued to walk around, trying to capture images of people in the rain. Because it was flooding and because I wasn't looking where I was going, I walked into a large sewage canal. I plunged in up to my waist in a rather disgusting liquid mix, lacerating an arm and leg and smashing a camera lens on the cement. Not only was I injured, but I was also embarrassed. I climbed slowly out, hoping no one had seen me. But two women had witnessed my plunge from the door of their simple one-room home. They came over, and obviously concerned about my well-being, started talking to me in Kreyòl. Without a translator, I just apologized that I couldn't speak their language (a phrase I often learn when working somewhere). They then started pulling me back behind the house, where they had some buckets of water they had carried on their heads from some far-off location. They then proceeded to pour two of the buckets of water over me, washing off the worst of the sewage. Any description of Haiti's people isn't complete unless we include their warmth, hospitality, and generosity.

Chris: There are so many, and I've tried to include a number in the book. Certainly, for me, being at the food cooperatives in northern Haiti was a wonderful experience: the mountains reminded me a bit of the foothills in Colorado, the state where I grew up, and there was a sense of hope there—and the fresh air didn't hurt.

As for one emblematic image: one that I didn't include in the book was from our assignment in January 2011. Paul and I, as well as our translator Ulrick and his cousin, who was our driver, were driving around near the port area in Port-au-Prince's Cité Soleil district. The images just kept cascading at me: people in the market, sorting through bundles of clothing, rummaging, just surviving, trying to get through the day. It was kind of overwhelming, and I thought of two friends back in New York who have never seen such poverty. I said to myself, "They would be absolutely shocked at this—the extent of poverty here."

What's next for Chris Herlinger and Paul Jeffrey?

Chris: I know that in coming years, my work for Church World Service will focus a bit more on themes related to nutrition and food security. As for other projects, another colleague with extensive experience in southern Sudan is talking to me about a possible collaboration on a history of the church's response to the decades-long civil war there. Nothing firm yet—just talk at this point. I'd also welcome another book collaboration with Paul. But as to what topic, or country, I have no idea. Sadly, I don't think there will be a shortage of ideas. Unfortunately, everything points to more disasters and serious problems in the world in the next few years.

Paul: I dunno what I'm doing next month!

Questions and Topics for Discussion

You may wish to open your discussion with prayer. The opening and closing prayers here are taken from *Women's Uncommon Prayers: Our Lives Revealed, Nurtured, Celebrated.*

Women of Haiti

what happens to women
who have no fuel
nothing to burn
who live on treeless slopes
barren to the sky
who walk in the sun
and sleep in the moon
unpatterned
dreaming of branches

—Ms. Lucy Germany

Rubble Nation

1. What did the title, *Rubble Nation*, evoke for you before you read the book? After you read it?
2. What preconceived notions did you bring to this book? Notions about the earthquake, about Haiti, about Haitians? In what way were you challenged?
3. How did the photos of Haiti after the earthquake influence your expectations/perceptions?

"There Is Still So Much to Do"

1. What do you think would constitute real "development" in Haiti? Who has the power to make it happen?
2. Disasters are a combination of natural threat and social vulnerability. What in Haiti's history made it more vulnerable to the seismic activity on January 12, 2010?

"On the Other Side" of the First Year

1. We give great weight to milestones like anniversaries. Why are arbitrary dates so important? What anniversaries do you look forward to? Which ones do you dread?

The Terrible Weight of Haiti's History

1. There is some evidence that President Jean-Bertrand Aristide's presidency was sabotaged by the U.S. government and by Haitian groups funded by U.S. government–funded groups like the International Republican Institute. If you are a U.S. citizen, how do you feel about one sovereign nation meddling in the affairs of another? What can you and your congregation do to change that kind of intervention?

2. One of the specific critiques of President Aristide was that, in his focus on the poor, he failed to reach out to all segments of society, importantly to the middle class. But his supporters stress he was finally able to give voice to the poor. How important is it to achieve consensus among a wide range of people, with vastly different needs and expectations? Can you think of occasions when the rich and middle class reached out to people on the margins of society?

In the Camps and on the Streets

1. When society breaks down, women and children are the most vulnerable to violence and exploitation. What role can churches play in protecting them? What has been the response in your church/community to protect and nurture women and children in crisis?

2. "Will I ever have a home again?" This is one of the most poignant questions a person could ask. Haiti is experiencing homelessness of a massive level. Yet even in a rich country like the U.S., many people are homeless or on the verge of homelessness. How should your community, your church respond to homeless people? How can you respond on an individual level?

3. Picture a person with no home to go to at the end of the day. Then picture a "homeless person." How does language affect the way you think about people struggling to survive at the edges of society?

4. How do you think about people who have lost their homes in the mortgage crisis?

The Reinvasion of the "Republic of NGOs"

1. The U.S. military—and militaries from around the world—played a significant role in the immediate aftermath of the quake. Yet humanitarian action and military response have traditionally been seen as separate activities, and humanitarian activists warn about overlapping or confused mandates. What do you think in general about military involvement in disaster response, and what particular challenges did U.S. military involvement pose in Haiti, which has a long history of U.S. intervention?

2. In the wake of the disaster, church relief groups and others raised hundreds of millions of dollars for use in Haiti. How has that money been spent? What lessons can we learn from the problems associated with this? And how can church groups and others move beyond traditional disaster response to work in *solidarity* with Haitian communities?

The Quest for Food Security

1. The issue of food security is entwined with the economic exploitation that has devastated Haiti. The policy of trade liberalization was disastrous for Haiti's ability to feed itself. Food co-ops in rural Haiti have had some success in making it possible for Haiti to take steps toward ensuring a regular food supply. What can people in urban areas do to get access to reasonably priced healthy food?
2. Haitians who could not support themselves on farms, as they had for generations, fled to the city, where they suffered economic exploitation. For example, clothing assembly plants have played a significant role in Haiti's recent economic history, and have made some members of the Haitian elite very wealthy. Keeping wages low in those plants has been a priority for the U.S. government. Do you own clothing or other articles manufactured in Haiti? What possibilities are there for purchasing fair-trade or other alternative products that contribute to sustainable economic growth in Haiti?

Haiti's God Talk

1. What's the impression you have had of voodoo, and how has the book made you rethink that?
2. How would you define liberation theology? What "real life" effect does it have in securing the well-being of a country?
3. Evangelical Christians have made tremendous inroads in Haiti. What does that branch of Christianity offer that mainline denominations do not?
4. It is natural to ask, in the face of tremendous upheaval, "How could God let this happen?" In the United Sates, the question was on everyone's lips after 9/11. How would you answer this question as an individual? As a member of the group?

Is Haiti Hopeless?

1. In *Rubble Nation*, we have read the stories and seen the photographs that lead us in many sad directions—despair, anger, helplessness—but there can be joy and hope found in unexpected places. How do you see Haiti's future? Can you think of ways to find "Haiti's Hope, Haiti's Promise"?

Prayer for Support

Jesus reach for me.
Spirit strengthen me.
God catch me.

—Mrs. Phoebe W. Griswold

Select Bibliography

Books

Aristide, Jean-Bertrand. *In the Parish of the Poor: Writings from Haiti*. Maryknoll, NY: Orbis Books, 1997.

Beckmann, David. *Exodus from Hunger: We are Called to Change the Politics of Hunger*. Louisville: Westminster John Knox Press, 2010.

Danner, Mark. *Stripping Bare the Body: Politics, Violence, War*. New York: Nation Books, 2009.

Danticat, Edwidge. "Claire of the Sea Light." From *Haiti Noir*. New York: Akashic Books. 2011.

El-Kati, Mahmoud. *Haiti: The Hidden Truth*. Brooklyn Park, MN: Papyrus Publishing, 2010.

Farmer, Paul. *The Uses of Haiti*. Monroe, ME: Common Courage Press, 1994.

Geitz, Elizabeth Rankin, Marjorie A. Burke, and Ann Smith, eds. *Women's Uncommon Prayers: Our Lives Revealed, Nurtured, Celebrated*. Harrisburg, PA: Morehouse Publishing. 2000.

Girard, Philippe. *Haiti: The Tumultuous History—from Pearl of the Caribbean to Broken Nation*. New York: Pallgrave Macmillon, 2010.

Greene, Graham. *The Comedians*. New York: Penguin Books, 2005.

Hallward, Peter. *Damming the Flood: Haiti and the Politics of Containment*. London: Verso Books, 2007.

Renda, Mary. *Taking Haiti: Military Occupation and the Culture of U.S. Imperialism 1915–1940*. Chapel Hill: University of North Carolina Press, 2001.

Schwartz, Timothy. *Travesty in Haiti: A True Account of Christian Missions, Orphanages, Food Aid, Fraud and Drug Trafficking*. Lexington, KY: BookSurge Publishing, 2010.

Wilentz, Amy. *The Rainy Season: Haiti—Then and Now*. New York: Simon & Schuster, 1989.

Magazines and Journals

Díaz, Junot. "Apocalypse: What Disasters Reveal." *Boston Review*, May/June 2011, www.bostonreview.net

Farmer, Paul. "An Anthropology of Structural Violence." The Sidney W. Mintz Lecture for 2001. *Current Anthropology*, Volume 45, Number 3, June 2004.

Herlinger, Chris. "Haiti: A Year Later." *Presbyterians Today*, March 2011.

Herlinger, Chris. "Hope Is Here in Haiti." *New World Outlook*, May/June 2011.

Herlinger, Chris. "Standstill in Haiti." *The Christian Century*, Aug. 9, 2010.

Jeffrey, Paul. "Nation Under Rubble: Women Struggle to Survive in Post-Quake Haiti." *Response*, May 2011.

News Services

Herlinger, Chris. "At Easter, Haitians Look Past the Quake toward 'the Life Ahead.'" Ecumenical News International (www.eni.ch), April 25, 2011.

Herlinger, Chris. "Haitian Clinics Battle Cholera While Facing Overwhelming Challenges." Catholic News Service (www.catholicnews.com), Feb.1, 2011.

Herlinger, Chris. "Haitians Mark a 'Very, Very Difficult Year.'" Ecumenical News International (www.eni.ch), Jan. 11, 2011.

Herlinger, Chris. "Six Months Later, Many in Haiti Feel 'It Just Happened.'" Ecumenical News International (www.eni.ch), July 12, 2010.

Newspapers

Herlinger, Chris. "After Presidential Elections, Haitians Weary of Easy Promises." *National Catholic Reporter*, April 27, 2011.

Herlinger, Chris. "Haitians Relieved 'to Be on the Other Side.'" *National Catholic Reporter*, Jan. 18, 2011.

Herlinger, Chris. "Pessimism Couples Hope for Change in Haiti." *National Catholic Reporter*, May 27, 2011.

Herlinger, Chris. "Quake Strained Haiti's Already Ailing Food System." *National Catholic Reporter*, Sept. 9, 2010.

Johnson, E. Thomas. "Haitians Still Wait for Recovery." *Los Angeles Times*, June 25, 2010, www.latimes.com

Mozingo, Joe. "Haitian quake shook leader to his core." Los Angeles Times, August 15, 2010, www.latimes.com

Sontag, Deborah. "In Haiti, the Displaced Are Left Clinging to the Edge." *The New York Times*, July 10, 2010, www.nytimes.com

Reports

McGuigan, Claire. "Agricultural Liberalization in Haiti." Christian Aid report, March 2006, http://www.christianaid.org.uk/Images/ca-agricultural-liberalisation.pdf

Spodek, Brent. "We Want To Know Why: Questioning Responsibility for Disasters." *AJWS Reports* (American Jewish World Service), Fall 2010, www.ajws.org

"You don't have to be there to help" from *Belief in Action: ACT Alliance Annual Report 2010*.

In addition, initial and follow-up stories from Haiti (2010–2011) by Chris Herlinger appeared on the websites of Church World Service (www.churchworldservice.org) and ACT Alliance (www.actalliance.org).